Borderland Churches

To Greg
For the faith we share....
The church we hope for...
The friendship we hold to...
Gary [illegible]
Jer. 29:4-9

The Columbia Partnership Leadership Series from Chalice Press

Christ-Centered Coaching: 7 Benefits for Ministry Leaders
Jane Creswell

Coaching for Christian Leaders: A Practical Guide
Linda J. Miller and Chad W. Hall

Courageous Church Leadership: Conversations with Effective Practitioners
John P. Chandler

Cultivating Perennial Churches
Robert D. Dale

Enduring Connections: Creating a Preschool and Children's Ministry
Janice Haywood

Evangelism Where You Live: Engaging Your Community
Stephen Pate and Gene Wilkes

Every Congregation Needs a Little Conflict
George W. Bullard Jr.

From the Outside In: Connecting to the Community Around You
Ronald W. Johnson

The Heart of the Matter: Changing the World God's Way
Charles Halley

Operation Inasmuch: Mobilizing Believers beyond the Walls of the Church
David W. Crocker

Pursuing the Full Kingdom Potential of Your Congregation
George W. Bullard Jr.

Reaching People under 40 while Keeping People over 60: Being Church to All Generations
Edward H. Hammett with James R. Pierce

Recreating the Church: Leadership for the Postmodern Age
Richard L. Hamm

Renew Your Congregation: Healing the Sick, Raising the Dead
Willliam T. McConnell

The Samaritan Way
David W. Crocker

Seeds for the Future: Growing Organic Leaders for Living Churches
Robert D. Dale

Spiritual Leadership in a Secular Age: Building Bridges Instead of Barriers
Edward H. Hammett

Borderland Churches

A Congregation's Introduction to Missional Living

Gary V. Nelson

CHALICE PRESS
ST. LOUIS, MISSOURI

Cover image: GettyImages

Cover and interior design: Elizabeth Wright

Visit Chalice Press on the World Wide Web at
www.chalicepress.com

10 9 8 7 6 5 4 3 2 1 08 09 10 11 12 13

Library of Congress Cataloging-in-Publication Data

Nelson, Gary E.
Borderland churches : a congregation's introduction to missional living / Gary Nelson.
p. cm.
ISBN 978-0-8272-0238-2
1. Mission of the church. 2. Church renewal. 3. Postmodernism–Religious aspects–Christianity. 4. Christian life. I. Title.
BV601.8.N36 2009
262'.001'7–dc22

2008044131

Printed in the United States of America

Contents

Acknowledgments

I was grateful for many reasons when George Bullard asked me to consider writing this book. It was an opportunity to gather the stories and concepts that have emerged out of my journey as a pastor and a periodic layperson in the church. For as long as I can remember, I have had a love for the church. It has not always been without disappointment, but, somehow, for me, church made sense. I have walked away from it, walked toward it, and wondered why my faith in Jesus required such commitment. It has never been easy, but it has always been important.

I have participated in congregations that have both challenged and inspired me to understand what church really could be. These places have helped me to see why God placed the church in the hands of a fragile and broken people. When we live as the church with stumbling courage, the power of God is displayed, as Paul said, in our weakness. That it needs to change to meet the challenge of its times is without question, but I have never been one to trash what has been, but rather desire to always discuss what must be. Each successive generation faces the challenge of building a new chapter from the chapter of the generation that preceded it. To ignore that we are standing on the shoulders of saints from the past is to be persons with little, if any, grasp of reality.

I have practiced ministry within a network of churches known as Canadian Baptists and I now serve them as their national and international ministries leader. It is probably a statement of the kind of people we are that they called me to be their General Secretary, as strange as that might seem. This proud group of churches is distinct in Canada for their diversity and their creativity. We have not always lived up to these possibilities, but when we do, we soar and are a remarkable people. I am proud to be part of this strange and wonderful tribe. I offer my sincere thanks to Mark, a good friend who is part of the tribe, for writing the foreword. His faithfulness to the pastoral task and his profound writings continue to challenge me.

The flavor of these strange and wonderful people is found at the CBM office. My colleagues–Terry, Blair, Sharlene, Carmin, Frank, and Jennifer–have supported me in this project. Gord and Harry read different incarnations of the manuscript and gave encouragement and suggestions over the journey of writing this book. Through a year of cancer treatment, Malcolm read my first musings and each successive edition while the chemo drip at the hospital did its thing. He has been an inspiration as he lived courageously in this time. He leaves to return to Kenya soon to continue this chapter in his life and ministry. Audrey cleaned up all my messy formatting and carelessness as she does so often while working alongside me.

I wrote this book with some people in mind. It was written for my father and mother, who nurtured my love for the church and who are challenged about what it means to be the church today. They do not always like what is going on in the present but they represent the faithful who over the years have served and ministered in churches as laypeople. I have used Mom as a sounding board by asking her to read sections of this book and respond. Thanks Mom!

Another person I had in mind as I wrote is my daughter Stacy. She lives with great dreams and plans, and has a faith that consistently inspires me. At first, I wanted to protect her when she told me that she was not going back to her teaching career after our grandson Garrett was born, and was instead taking a position with her church in outreach ministry. I have since learned instead that she is quite capable of taking care of herself and that her instincts for ministry are marvelous. To her husband Phil who loves her dearly–thank you.

Mostly this book has been written because Carla, my best friend and lover, has always encouraged me to write. She believes in me more than I believe in myself and I have been blessed by our life together. The way she thinks and her deep concern for people are the fuel of our borderland living. Sometimes I stand back and watch her in places such as Kenya, where she is known as Muthongoi Ndanu (leader who brings joy wherever she goes), and I marvel at the gift she has been. Her call is now to teach teachers to be true to their vocation. To those who are encouraging Christians to leave the public schools, I would challenge them to an hour of discussion with her, for she has served faithfully, redemptively, and richly for many years as a follower of Christ in that setting. She has always been a borderland dweller. Her ability to know my mind has made this book better. Her life with me has made ministry exciting and a shared experience. She knows me and I am grateful and alive in that knowing. Thank you Carla.

Gary V. Nelson
Toronto, Canada

Editor's Foreword

Inspiration and Wisdom for Twenty-First–Century Christian Leaders

You have chosen wisely in deciding to study and learn from a book published in **The Columbia Partnership Leadership Series** with Chalice Press. We publish for

- Congregational leaders who desire to serve with greater faithfulness, effectiveness, and innovation.
- Christian ministers who seek to pursue and sustain excellence in ministry service.
- Members of congregations who desire to reach their full kingdom potential.
- Christian leaders who desire to use a coach approach in their ministry.
- Denominational and parachurch leaders who want to come alongside affiliated congregations in a servant leadership role.
- Consultants and coaches who desire to increase their learning concerning the congregations and Christian leaders they serve.

The Columbia Partnership Leadership Series is an inspiration- and wisdom-sharing vehicle of The Columbia Partnership, a community of Christian leaders who are seeking to transform the capacity of the North American church to pursue and sustain vital Christ-centered ministry. You can connect with us at www.TheColumbiaPartnership.org.

Primarily serving congregations, denominations, educational institutions, leadership development programs, and parachurch organizations, the Partnership also seeks to connect with individuals, businesses, and other organizations seeking a Christ-centered spiritual focus.

We welcome your comments on these books, and we welcome your suggestions for new subject areas and authors we ought to consider.

George W. Bullard Jr., Senior Editor
GBullard@TheColumbiaPartnership.org

The Columbia Partnership,
332 Valley Springs Road, Columbia, SC 29223-6934
Voice: 803.622.0923, www.TheColumbiaPartnership.org

Foreword

Few things are sadder than an aging rock star in the throes of a comeback. Molting, paunchy, jowly, pulling muscles and cracking notes, it's an act of self-caricature. It was in that spirit that the historian Felipe Fernandez-Armesto described the death of Elvis, just as he was becoming a parody of himself, as a "great career move."

Which has nothing to do with this foreword, except this: the church sometimes behaves like an aging rock star in the throes of a comeback. We remember what we once were, and dream we can be it once more. With a face-lift, a tummy-tuck, a hairpiece, and a new sound, we might just draw a crowd again.

We've been trying that for a while now. Some of the results border on self-parody.

Gary Nelson has a better idea. He writes *Borderland Churches: A Congregation's Introduction to Missional Living* at once to awaken us, to inspire us, and to help us navigate the real changes needed if we're to be on a mission with God. He calls us to face the new reality–our abar moment, he calls it, a crossing over, when we leave behind our nostalgic reveries of a world long gone and enter into the world we actually inhabit: pluralistic, post-Christian and, above all, brimming with opportunity. But Gary also equips us for that crossing over. He does this by recapturing the biblical substance of the church–a community called out, called together, called for, and called to–which must live faithfully at the borderlands of culture, that precarious but exhilarating place where faith and other faiths and no faith meet.

A few years ago I spent time with Gary in Kenya. We traveled together, visited churches, and talked sometimes late into the night. I had the privilege of listening to Gary teach, every day for two weeks, a group of Kenyan pastors and church leaders. Mostly, he taught about leading borderland churches, the theme of this book. What struck me as I watched those leaders–listening with riveted attention, taking copious notes, interacting vigorously–is that Gary is speaking a word for his time and place, but also for every time and place. He is not merely promoting the latest fashion in methodology. He's imparting enduring wisdom.

And it's not just a message for leaders. Gary writes, not for some elite priestly guild, but for the priesthood of all believers. He's writing for those men and women who make up our churches–who sit on its

committees, pay its bills, and teach its children–and who daily seek practical, biblical ways to be faithful to her deepest, truest, holiest purposes. This is simply the book to put in their hands.
And lucky you: now it's in yours.

Prepare to cross over.
Shalom

Mark Buchanan
Pastor & Author

Introduction

On this particular occasion, a variety of people from across Canada and the United States had gathered to discuss postmodernism. It was a time long before the "p" word had become fashionable and we had come together to explore its implications on the church and its mission. While several in attendance at those meetings have become the gurus of this discussion and subsequent discussions around the emerging church, I was there to offer a perspective from the local church. I was a pastor of a renewing downtown congregation and one who continually felt slightly out of synch with the way church was being "done" around me.

It was not a lack of admiration on my part. There were several successful models around me that were being effective in their context. Nor was it personal insecurity. It was simply that our congregation did not fit. This messy mix of diverse people was probably postmodern before postmodern became the buzzword. The majority who gathered at this old downtown church had little if any connection to church until they arrived in our sanctuary. We were doing this "liturgical worship thing" which seemed profoundly out of touch with what others were doing with worship teams and PowerPoint presentations, yet we were growing. Nobody could figure out why, including me.

At that conference, I spoke with one of the sages of the discussion about the church in the twenty-first century. He too was a pastor and so we began a discussion typical of most pastoral dialogues. We talked about our churches. Gratefully, we did not start at the peacock stage of comparing the beauty of our tails' plumage (translated: size of church, worship attendance, and number of pastoral staff). It was much more genuine and vulnerable than that. We were struggling to understand what we were facing.

At one point, I asked him to articulate the challenges he was facing in his ministry. His answer was quick and pointed because it came out of an encounter that had taken place with his board of elders just the week prior. "One of my challenges is that many of our people listen to Charles Stanley and wish that I preached like him. What is yours?"

I must confess to being puzzled for a moment. Please excuse my cultural ignorance, but I, at the time, did not know who Charles

Stanley was. After telling me about Charles Stanley, he asked again, "what are your challenges?"

My answer was also quick. It too came out of the immediacy of my experience. My experience of ministering to this diverse crew of people often left me wishing it could just be "normal"–a place where attendance was sure and language, rhythms and ethos recognizable to that in which I had grown up. This was not the case and so I answered his query with an equally passionate retort, "My biggest challenge is that none of the people in my church would know who Charles Stanley is, and, frankly, if they heard him, as you have described, they probably wouldn't like him."

A Canadian, Eh?

You should know that I am a Canadian writing in Canada. At first glance, that may not seem all that important until you realize that, as Canadians, we live in a country in which a deep cultural marginalization of the church has been taking place for years. Religious affiliation in Canada is a private matter not to be publicly expressed. In fact, if our politicians have church affiliation, they are marked as "not to be trusted."

We Canadians pride ourselves on our multicultural mosaic. Our diversity creates a hyphenated way of living in which everyone is something else: Scottish-Canadian, Indo-Canadian, and so on. This idea of mosaic, as opposed to the idea of a melting pot, appreciates the differences often in very superficial ways (i.e., food, fashion, and festivals) while missing the deeper cultural values and beliefs at work. We have never quite understood where religion and faith fit, except as privately held idiosyncrasies.

The government of Canada performs a national census every ten years to monitor changes in population and trends in our country. Data recently released described a growing apathy toward religious institutions in the hearts and minds of Canadian people and, at the same time, a growing spiritual sensitivity.

The findings are fascinating. Most striking is that 16 percent of all Canadians checked the category labeled "no religion." Think about that. Out of every one hundred people, sixteen felt that it was important to check the little box on the census sheet that said, "no religion." What is even more sobering is that 40 percent of all those people were under the age of twenty-four.

This marginalization of the church is just beginning to take place south of the Canadian border, but in Canada, it is already woven into the fabric of society. Canadians are not angry at the church–they simply do not care about it. They are extremely spiritual in their searching–over 80 percent of all Canadians say they believe in God–but almost the same percentage of people also acknowledge they do not believe in the church. We are a country of genuine spiritual inquiry and religious institutional rejection all wrapped into one.

Canadians search spiritually in unprecedented ways but are certain that loyal, well-meaning organized churchgoers will not understand their search. It is an interesting place to live as a person of faith, and one that challenges the assumptions and frameworks of what and how we live as the church.

We Are Where You Are Going!

My involvement with colleagues and peers in the United States has helped me to realize that often what they are describing as the changing landscape of church life in America is in truth what we Canadians have already experienced. David Fitch says, "Canada may be a snapshot of the post-Christian conditions that lie immediately ahead of the United States."[1]

Living in these cultural and religious realities has been good for the church in Canada. We have been forced to think about how to engage and talk as people of faith in a world that is no longer wired "Christendom friendly." To those living in the United States, we in Canada are like a time-lapse camera, giving you a future picture of where you are going. I have no desire to sound like a cranky prophet. This is more of an invitation to learn from one another in new ways.

Looking for the "Magic Key"

In response to this growing marginalization of the church, we Canadian clergy did what seemed logical. We looked for successful models and tried to implement them in our contexts. This did work in some instances. There were and are churches growing in Canada using models developed elsewhere. At least they seem to work for a time. However, these growing churches appear to do little to stem the tide of decline and cultural ineffectiveness.

So, we continued with what still seemed logical. We searched the numerous books, seminars, and workshops on the church. We studied particular models, mostly from the U.S. These different events fed our desire as well-meaning clergy and lay leaders to enter the search for the "magic key." You know the magic key. It is a way of thinking, a methodological approach that will unlock the secrets to successful and effective church life and relieve us of our sense of inadequacy.

We are grateful for the models presented over the last decades. To be fair, none of them promised to be the "magic key." But we hoped they would be. We gained some insights, but mostly we continued the sacred quest for the grail of effectiveness. In our cynical moments, we wondered if the new models were simply retreads of how we used to do church. In our more hopeful moments, we were encouraged in the possibilities. And in our realistic moments, we posed the question, "what if there is no magic key?"

Listening to an Emerging Dialogue

It is out of this context that a dialogue has begun to take place, first among a number of urban ministry people, and, over the past several years, among different circles of clergy and laity. Many of the conversations were disconnected from each other, but we realized that while we might be using different words, we were thinking about the same themes.

The conversation is focused on the practice of ministry by taking the church into the streets, neighborhoods, and workplaces. The energy of the dialogue is founded in the belief that we must move from "come to" to "go to" models of being the church.

It emerged from the intuitive feelings of clergy and laity alike that change needed to happen. In our worst moments, we wondered if church was worth fighting for anymore. And, at other times, we feared that we were simply playing at it. This stems out of a deep abiding love for the church and the belief that something drastically different must take place.

It has been a discovery of the missional nature of the church, but the shift started taking place long before the concept was unpacked. Canadian church leaders asked, "what might effectively reach our culture with the gospel? What does it mean to be the church?" We were asking questions out of a serious realization that nips and tucks around already existing models would no longer be adequate for the challenge of the times.

Embracing a Missional Mind-set

As a starting point in the new emerging reality, we must embrace what might be called "a ministry of inconvenience." This is a required attitudinal change in most churches. No matter how well we understand the times we are in, it is impossible to be effective as the church without crossing boundaries of comfort, culture, and convenience. The average person on Sunday morning is not waking up and thinking about what church he or she should attend. These people know that they have seemingly much more intriguing and urgent things to do with their time. No amount of attractive programming is going to woo them back.

One of my friends, a new believer, once told me that the most difficult habit that he had to break was to stop going for early brunch on Sunday morning. On the way to church on Sunday morning, a left turn at a certain intersection promised Belgian waffles. He told me that 75 percent of the time he turned right but it was a tough decision. He was brought to faith and to church through relationships nurtured outside the walls of the church. Those relationships were only possible because of a church that affirmed through words and deeds that those places of relationship outside of the church were important.

We are discovering, or perhaps rediscovering, the mission agenda of the church where we, as followers of Jesus Christ, see ourselves not simply as a "called together" people but also as "called out" people. This mandate must capture our imagination. God calls us to live a missionary existence in the world not just as something we do, such as education and worship, but as the very essence and character of the church.

This sounds reasonable enough. However, romanticizing this call to be "sent" is not helpful. Missionary life is full of inconvenience and discomfort. It will require that we work outside of ourselves. It will require that we substitute "that which is comfortable to us" for "that which will be comfortable for you."

Living in the Borderlands

My colleague Frank Byrne has been a great help to me. One day, while facilitating at a staff training event, he introduced the captivating idea of "borderlands." He told us that the life of mission was lived in the "borderlands" and described these as places where "faith and unfaith intersect." We have since expanded this understanding. In a global world, the borderlands are actually the places where "Christian faith, other faiths, and unfaith intersect." That day, Frank emphasized the profound difference between mission and ministry. Mission is always lived in the borderlands.

The idea of borderlands caught my imagination. It helped clarify my deep belief in the church and its call to live incarnationally and genuinely in the world. My friend Mark Buchanan has used the borderland metaphor in a very different way. He believes that we have constructed a God of our own making–a God who is way too safe. A

God who is unpredictable and "holy wild" is not to our liking so we run to a place Mark calls "borderland," a strange and safe place that promises nothing and delivers nothing. He calls us as followers of Jesus to escape this borderland and live with God in "the holy wild."[2]

Gloria Anzaldúa, in her book *Borderlands/La Frontera,* writes from a literal and geographic borderland: the United States–Mexico border. She uses the borderland metaphor to describe a place where people of different ethnicities occupy the same territory and where the space between these cultures shrinks with intimacy. In the borderlands the context demands people become new beings.[3]

Henry Giroux writes of the need for educators to create conditions in which students can become border crossers. It is a way to understand the mingling of multiple cultures, languages, histories, and identities. We cross borders either "to expand or to shrink the connectedness among individuals, groups and places."[4]

For me, the idea of borderlands provides a helpful way of understanding where ministry should take place. It is that strange place of engagement where the "holy wild" God is encountered in risky borderland living. I believe that this idea of "borderlands" can provide a metaphorical framework that allows us to imagine what the missional church life looks like.

I have come to see it in this way. The fullness of the missionary existence of the church was lost sometime in history. Contemporary churches live "boundaried" lives, encamping on their side of the borders and living out a mission life of illusion and limited action. The illusion is sustained by an approach to missions expressed only as "over there." The funding of paid missionaries and, now, the popular short-term mission trips became ways to live that missionary existence. We either fund people to live the missional life full time or we live it out ourselves. Sadly, we too often miss the borderland missionary call in our everyday worlds.

Still, the mission instinct endures. As a result, under the title of outreach, we build metaphorical observational towers to study the trends and cultural behaviors. We listen to people just like us describe the borderlands. These observers are granted immense authority whether or not their observations emerge from having actually experienced the borderlands. The information we receive allows us to adapt to what we believe to be more "culturally appropriate" ministry. We prepare to receive people from the other side of the borders. We hope that they may venture into our territory. When they do, we know we are ready because we have read the books and we have made the cosmetic changes necessary for borderland people to feel comfortable in our strange world.

Churches alter their styles of worship, change their dress codes, and shape their congregational life in perceived courageous revolutionary acts. However, cosmetic or organizational changes, no matter how radical they may appear to the Christian culture, have minimal impact. We still are waiting for "them" to come to "us."

More creative churches develop strategic teams and programs that move across the borders with concentrated and well-intentioned desires to encounter borderland people. This simulated "subversive activity" is designed to bring people into the fold while requiring insignificant amounts of change on the part of the Christian subculture.

Both of these orientations ensure that churches remain relatively comfortable and that changes are more cosmetic than revolutionary. Their movement is still within the walls of the church. The only people truly "crossing-over" are those who are sufficiently adventurous and courageous to explore other territory. They also confirm that while congregations know that things need to change, they would prefer that change not create any discomfort.

If effective mission emerges from inconvenience and discomfort, then the borderlands symbolize this struggle. It is here that we are challenged by the differences of others. Living in the borderlands allows us to become learners struggling, as did the missionaries of the past, with our cultural constructs concerning church and Christian living. The borderlands stretch our thinking and challenge us to sort out the negotiables; to understand what is cultural baggage and what is truly essential and biblical. It is here where we find the humble sensibility to deepen in our engagement with others. The church becomes the church in the borderlands and faith becomes real in the engagement.

The idea of the church living into the community is captivating churches. Conversations with clergy and laity alike have drastically changed. Studying the culture is not enough. They want to engage it, to move beyond being simply seeker-sensitive or relevant to postmoderns in their ministry. They want to become communities of faith genuinely encountering people not inclined to church. They want to struggle and be personally challenged by living their faith in the borderlands where "Christian faith, other faiths, and unfaith intersect." We have much to learn, but we are on the journey. This is not just another model; it is a way of visioning the church and its mission. In truth, it is recapturing a fundamental belief about church.

Emerging Places of Borderland Living

A few years ago, I became the head of our denomination's international and national mission organization. This position has afforded me the privilege of visiting churches across North America. These opportunities have provided an exposure that gives even more shape to this idea of borderlands and to the ideas presented in this book. I have begun to call "borderland churches" those congregations journeying to something very different.

These borderland churches are unsettling. Their commitment to discipleship, vibrant worship, and community life is costly, taking ministry and mission to a level beyond simple loyalty to committees and church life. They measure effectiveness and success with different standards, standards that are not typical to church structures.

Borderland churches are not always the largest churches in the area. They are not necessarily the most creative, but they have an energy that is absolutely compelling. They are creative, but it is not their creativity that captures you. It is the impact they are having on their communities that startles you.

People of borderland churches live on the edge. They take chances. They are passionate about reaching out into their community, and they are willing to venture out of their comfort zones. Their leaders have opened themselves up to the possibilities of God doing new things both in their church and in themselves. They are unfinished products, on an adventure of discovery toward what it means to be the church in the twenty-first century.

By becoming borderland churches, they are willing to become genuine communities where people can come as they are and start growing into something else. They realize that the relational aspect of ministry is crucial to effective community engagement.

They have a very different way of life together. Their community is genuine and "real." Borderland churches are not discovering a new way of being the church. They are discovering the core essential quality of what it has always meant to be the church.

Borderland Friendly Leaders

The borderland church will have implications for its leadership. What happens if church leaders are not missionaries? What happens if they are not borderland friendly? If they have not experienced borderland living, how will they mobilize people for engagement, not only *inside* the church where they worship but also in the places where they live? How do leaders challenge people to borderland living if their own lives are programmed for Christian subculture?

It will be impossible to lead others to places of effective missionary engagement if we, as leaders, are uncomfortable in the borderlands. Borderland living for the church requires catalyst leaders who are more than pastoral caregivers or great visionaries. They live what they teach. Charles Van Engen writes, "Merely developing authority–only telling what they should do and devising programs to do it–will not be enough to mobilize."[5] It is my conviction that a key catalytic feature of borderland churches is that their leaders are able to live and thrive in the borderlands. They are comfortable in their cultural contexts and able to relate genuinely to the "unfaithed." Christian leaders must become borderland friendly. But how?

Maybe they need to do what Jesus did. He hung out with borderland people even though he was always criticized for doing so. The religious establishment was incensed but he lived alongside them anyway. Maybe it is time that we become more Christlike and hang out in the borderlands more often. Join a club, a community sports league, or maybe simply spend time outside of the office with the people with whom you work. Get involved in your community by being a part of the life of the place.

A friend of mine in an urban Italian neighborhood has been criticized for joining a cycling club because the club meets on prayer meeting night. Yet over the last months, my friend has had more meaningful faith exploration conversations than ever in his ministry.

Another pastor spends every Saturday night, not preparing his sermon, but playing hockey with a bunch of borderland people who pump him with questions around faith at the after-game celebrations. He has even raised money from this group for projects in the church.

A church leader in the Midwest spends two days a week at the curling club in the small town that he serves as a pastor. Everyone in the community comes to the curling club at some time in the week during the winter. It is the "borderland" of his small community and the place where he has learned to become borderland friendly.

Two lay leaders and a pastor from a small church engaged in its community meet with local and national political leaders to encourage them to build a community club in the area. They know these politicians by name and have met with them on other community issues.

A chief investigator and fingerprint expert with the police force in Nairobi started talking with his fellow workers at the police headquarters and, from those conversations, seven people began a Bible study. Now over two hundred colleagues meet two times a week in the morning before work to study scripture. It only happened because he was serious about living as a person of faith in the borderlands.

LET THE DISCOVERY BEGIN

Where are your borderlands? What would it take for you to become borderland friendly? This book is written...

- For those who live or desire to live in these borderland places where Christian faith, other faiths, and unfaith are in continual and creative dialogue.
- For people who want to walk with this next generation who seem to understand that borderland living must take place.
- For those people who have searched for "magic keys" and are now realizing that more than tinkering is required.
- For those who, even after reading all the books on postmodernism, realize that, no matter how deeply you grasp the complexities of the times and culture, a radical shift attitudinally will need to take place.

This book is written not to present a model but to help us recapture our missional existence, encouraging one another to lives of faith in places that we have come to fear.

1

Learning to Sing the Song

BORDERLAND COMPASS POINT

The drastic changes that have occurred since the last century's North American cultural religious acceptance of today's secular environment demands that the church rediscover its ministry and mission. Psalm 137 offers insight into the challenge of "singing a new song" in the world to which God has called His people.

In the early nineties, I began my tenure as pastor of an "Old First Church" in Western Canada. For the previous thirty years, it had bled people. There were numerous reasons for its decline. Changes in the neighborhood, sociological shifts of suburban growth, and simple theological drift were all factors. It was painfully obvious that this once proud downtown congregation had become a shell of its past in size and influence.

The challenge of renewal brought me to that place along with the distinct feeling that I needed to experience things about which I had been preaching. Young and energetic, I had most recently been the director of an urban ministry training center where we studied and taught the skills necessary for ministry in the city context. A growing sense of being too young to be an expert and the need to test the concepts about which I had been teaching made me open to a call back to pastoral ministry. So, when this old downtown congregation contacted me, it appeared the perfect place for practicing what I had been teaching. I responded to the call but, within the first months, a deep sense of despair enveloped me, due in part to the presence of one of the church's former ministers.

He had been the minister of the church in the 1950s. During his tenure, a Canadian national news magazine called *Star Weekly* sent a reporter across the nation over a six-month period to discover the top ten preachers in Canada. This former minister was chosen as one of them.

My awareness of that award became difficult to forget. Over my years as pastor of this same church, until the time of his death, this great man and accomplished pastor managed to mention this accolade to me in almost every one of our encounters.

This former pastor from the days of the church's glory had just moved back to the city to settle into retirement and rejoined the church. His prior success, albeit thirty years earlier, gave him great confidence to judge that my approach to ministry was wrong. This confident belief fueled a mission for his declining years. He would take me under his tutelage, inform me on a continual basis of my pastoral shortcomings and lead me into the promised land, as defined by his view of ministry.

Every visit to his apartment induced emotional pain. My ego and my energy were drained. Through it all, he portrayed an amazing intuitive ability to discern the Achilles heel of my confidence. He ended each visit with the same refrain. "Gary, did you know that in 1955 I was named one of the top ten preachers in Canada by *Star Weekly*?" I braced myself for what was coming next, "Gary, have you ever been named one of the top ten preachers in Canada?"

I confess that I too often left these encounters seething. As I returned to my car, my mind would be spinning with an array of eloquent and pointed replies that I was determined to use the next visit. Some were gentle; others, cruel. I never did use them even though my quiver is still full. They did provide solace in my frustration and pain. It was not just that *Star Weekly* no longer exists as a magazine in Canada. It was also, more importantly, that this predecessor did not realize that in the times in which I was ministering no one even cared who the top ten preachers in Canada were.

We Aren't in Kansas Anymore, Toto!

We live in different times than the ones that this competent and talented clergyperson knew. It is no longer 1955, when 68 percent of Canadians attended a place of worship on a weekly basis. More Canadians attended church per capita than in the United States. It is a marvel to think of a time when the instinct for the majority of Canadians was to get up on a Sunday morning and go to church. That was what people did in 1955.

Now, church attendance on a given Sunday in Canada is more like 13 percent. In some urban settings, it is even much lower. The institutional religious world has been drastically altered. Now pastors live and seek to lead effectively in a time when more people consider brunch the activity of choice for Sunday morning.

A discussion around the changing environment of culture and religious institutional life caused an older respected patriarch of our denomination to muse about ministry and its beginnings. He paused for a moment and then said, "Boy, I am so glad that I am not starting ministry now!" It was an amazing comment made by someone who had been very effective in the old paradigm. Somehow he grasped the complexity and vulnerability of the altered landscape of culture and society and its subsequent impact on the mission and ministry of the church.

Many effective and successful clergy persons from that old paradigm would be challenged to make sense of the new realities. Theirs was a time in which assumptions and positional authority were rarely challenged. It was simpler. A preacher could stand in the pulpit and wait for people to show up. To be one of the top ten preachers in the country meant something both inside and outside of the church. It still has some meaning in the United States, but, even there, it is waning into an in-house affirmation.

The visits with my predecessor continue to serve as a watershed story for my ministry journey to this point. It captures and mirrors the experienced realities we face in the North American church of the twenty-first century–experienced realities not always appreciated beyond cultural observation.

Profound shifts and alterations have taken place in North American society over the last few decades. Many want to label those changes with words such as *secularization* and *postmodernism*. Labels can be helpful, but they need to be unpacked. Their emotional experiences rather than their conceptual frames need attention. Like Dorothy looking around the new world to which a tornado has transported her, "We aren't in Kansas anymore." It is no longer 1955–or, for that matter 1975 or 1995–and the hope to return to "Kansas" is a futile dream. Kansas no longer exists.

Singing the Song in the Borderland

Our experience is similar to that of the writer of Psalm 137. Ripped out of the familiar world of Jerusalem, the psalmist has been dragged to Babylon's vastly different world. The strange new rhythms of life, frameworks of beliefs, and foundations of relationships assault his sensibilities. A constant taunting is going on around him by those who know the comforting winds of the place in which he now lives.

They call to him. Maybe they challenge the seeming inconsequential nature of his past religious experience. "Come on, sing us one of those songs from Zion" Translation: "I dare you, sing one of those good old songs from your past. You know the song, the one that is meaningless!"

The anguish in the psalmist's refrain is palpable. Out of a deep sense of dislocation and sadness he cries, "How do I sing the songs of Zion in a foreign land?" Translation: "How do I sing my song of faith here in this new world?"

There it is. This is the common experience of faithful people and churches in the present, those desiring to be conscientious and effective followers of Jesus Christ. They must face with honesty and transparency the impact at a cultural and community level. But it is not easy. Realizing the profound shifts that have made this world so different, they cry out, "How do we do this church thing in these strange times?" This is the journey that we all must take before we truly find our song for this time.

Singing the Song of the Past

If you grew up in church and remember a joyful past, then you will recognize the first stage in the journey. With melodramatic passion the psalmist remembers his past Jerusalem experiences and pledges his loyalty to that time and place. It sounds so familiar. Longtime members of the church, facing difficult times in the present, look back and remind each other how good it used to be. "Wasn't it great when pastor so-and-so was here? My, he/she could preach." "Do you remember how Reverend what's-his-name filled our sanctuary worship service twice every Sunday?" "Youth used to flock to our programs on Friday night." "The Sunday school attendance was such that we had to build new facilities. We had classes all over the church, even in the sanctuary." "Do you remember when we first went to contemporary worship? People came from other places just to be part of what was happening." "The pastor did it all by himself."

Let us be honest. The past always seems better than it was in reality. It may have been very good, but the factors that made it possible are rarely discussed. The past has a way of refining and refinishing the rougher raw edges that truly existed. My parents, for example, remember my childhood in elementary school much better than it really was. It was a time of great difficulty for me. My grade four teacher, in consultation with specialists, placed me on a program designed to help modify my behaviors, which were disrupting the class. My devoted mother has kindly forgotten this. I put her through years of very difficult parent/principal meetings. That the principal in grade six was forced to place me at the back of the class, away from others, is written off as the act of a woman who "did not like little boys." Memory has a wonderful way of forgetting.

Remembering, however, is important. It fuels the present by giving us a foundational experience. Many passages in the scriptures call us to "remember." The problem occurs when those memories are romanticized and used as a rod to measure the present. They become a way of denying the reality of change in the present and a way of distracting oneself from the implications for change.

Sing a Song of Anger

The psalmist moves from melodramatic remembering to a more destructive response. Frustrated with the strangeness of this world and, in the midst of his powerlessness to sing into it, he gets angry. The last verses of this psalm are raw. They portray an anger that, when unleashed, becomes destructive. It is not reasonable and it certainly is far from rational. This cornered, religiously committed person just wants revenge.

So, he lashes out with the emotions of a surrounded wild beast with no apparent escape route. This new world frightens him and the results of this unsettledness are words full of spite and bitterness. These words even wish for destruction on the children of this strange world.

People in church can sound very much like the psalmist. They can feel trapped in strange worlds that they cannot sing into. Their responses can appear unfeeling and angry. Christians speak vile words everyday, out of feelings of powerlessness and fear. They desperately seek to engage the threatening issues, but their words are surprisingly unlike those of Jesus. The terrible signs of protest over the issues of sexual orientation or words spoken at times by the political right are far outside the law of love set down by Jesus. Sometimes we need to make a stand, but never one that attacks.

Church fights can often spiral out of control. They emerge in the life of the congregation as a natural extension of community, but too often escalate into personal attacks. When they become personal, they invariably escalate transforming the conflict into destructive relational and emotional tirades.

Times Have Changed

Psalm 137 captures with a genuine humanness the church's journey into the twenty-first century. It almost borders on the ridiculous to tell someone that times have changed. We experience change on a daily basis. New questions are being asked about sexual orientation, marriage, the family, and lifestyles in general. We are increasingly aware that a daily trip to Starbucks requires a financial transaction greater than the daily income of 40 percent of the world's population. Terrorism events from New York to the Middle East burst the bubble of North American existence; the appearance of being safe and secure has disappeared. Of course, we are now living an existence that most people around the world have lived for many years, but it has changed our world and that seems to be what matters to most of us. Some eager souls may want to deal with this new emerging world, but, for most of us, fear grips.

Some of these changes feel like they have been imposed. We did not have choice so, why should we embrace this new reality? We did not ask or wish for this strange world in which we live. Why even learn the new song?

These are interesting but unrealistic questions. We seem to hold to the mistaken idea that everything around us can dramatically shift without requiring any adaptive movement on our part. It is inherently illogical, yet this is exactly what many of us do. We seem to think that church expressions are nailed down for all time. The way we have previously experienced church is the way that it should continue to be. Even worse is the mistaken idea that it will only take a few cosmetic changes to appear "contemporary" and relevant.

Fearing the Unknown

The intensity of the man's anger when he confronted me after the service surprised me. After completing my sermon as the guest preacher in his church, he immediately came up to me after the service: "We haven't changed this worship service since 1929." The theme of my sermon had focused on the need to learn to sing a new song, given the changes occurring around us. He was not interested in this new song. He was convinced that the old one was quite fine. Unfortunately, like many of us, he thought this was a debate about singing hymns or choruses. It would be wonderful if it were that simple.

The depth of his emotions and the intensity of the expression on his face startled me. He was livid. Fear of the present and the anxiety produced by required or even imagined modifications struck terror in him. Knowing how to sing and realizing that the song may need to be different does not necessarily move naturally to singing the song that needs to be sung. In fact, if you are at all anxious about change, it may cause you to desire to dig in and sing the old song even louder.

I wanted to understand the tensions he was feeling so I probed just a bit. "Has anything else in your life *not* changed since 1929?" I asked. He was obviously startled by the question, and for a moment, stepped back in silence. Then with stammering and quivering lips, he replied, "No." My reply came quickly and with the desire for him to reflect deeply on the fact of the change around him. I said to him, "If that is true, then it might be a good idea to think about what that means for your church."

Learning to sing in this strange time has little to do with choruses or hymns. The cosmetic worship changes of the last decades of church life, while at times helpful, have also proven distracting. The desire to be more appealing and relevant in the rhythms of our worship to those who live in the borderlands is genuine. For some churches, altering our songs of worship was the beginning of a journey toward relevance and impact. However, the worship wars of the last two decades of the twentieth century were moments of trivial pursuit. They placed simplistic and shallow characteristics on people outside the influence of the church, making it sound too often as if borderland people were simply sitting at home on Sunday waiting for us as the church to change our worship style. If it only changed, they would come.

If we seek to engage people in meaningful dialogue, we must engage them at deeper levels. Borderland people are not superficial. They are unlikely to be drawn into our world by the simple alteration of our music. Your next-door neighbor is not likely to be asking why you don't sing choruses. People searching spiritually are not agonizing about the hardness of our pews. Many of them are simply living in the sincere belief that they have found a much more meaningful way to live their lives on Sunday, let alone Monday and beyond.

The song we must learn to sing is much more profound than a chorus or a hymn. It is about attitudes and presuppositions. It is also atmosphere where we offer genuine community and authentic relationships. The song seeks to answer the question of what it means to be the church relevantly in this context and these times. Trapped in our memories, we will only hinder the sense of urgency required to initiate change.

Developing a Sense of Urgency

Light bulb changing jokes float incessantly over the Internet. It makes you wonder if people have too much time on their hands.

"How many psychologists does it take to change a light bulb?" "Just one, but the light bulb has to really *want* to change." Another one goes, "How many congregational people does it take to change a light bulb?" "Change???"

For all the words and images we conjure up for facing our reality, the most difficult truth is that we will never learn to sing the new song if we do not feel the urgency to do so. Strange as it may seem, many do not feel any urgency at all.

John Kotter, a professor from Harvard School of Business, agrees. In his book *Leading Change*, Kotter states that the greatest hindrance to needed change in any organization is a lack of urgency.[1] He studied a variety of organizations that were obviously struggling but seemingly unable to make the required changes necessary to embrace their new realities. Complacency, he discovered, was an entrenched atmosphere and behavior for almost everyone. To his surprise, no one appeared to ask if there was a better way. No one seemed to grasp how critical the situation was. He explored further and was surprised that little disturbance or agitation was felt about the status quo and, as a result, very little urgency was felt about addressing the needed changes.

In fact, to his surprise, standards were lowered and measurements of effectiveness were even altered to better represent the present situation. It reminded me of a well-meaning person in a declining congregation who told me, "It isn't that people are leaving our church, they just aren't coming." Somehow she thought this would help me understand why it was not their fault that they were declining as a church.

Kotter noted that in these companies, negative feedback was often ignored and, oddly as it seems, praise of the status quo was celebrated. Companies went a long way to ensure that the risky nature of the future was affirmed in such a way as to guarantee the organization would decide to stay the course. Going slow in an age of rapid change is simply a way of making sure that change will not happen and that the song will not be sung. The most important element for healthy change in any organization is urgency.

A deep unsettling questioning of reality always precedes congregational renewal and transformation. People only act in a transformational way when they feel urgency. Unfortunately, complacency is a deeply rooted attitude. We ignore the realities around us, take counsel only from ourselves, and listen to only what we want to hear. We wring our hands with anxiety, but continue to ignore signs pointing in the new direction. The song needs to be sung in a new way, but we naively hold on to the way it was.

More than Tinkering

"Change for change's sake is not always good." I don't know why my colleague needed to tell me this in our morning discussion over coffee. It seemed important to her. We were discussing the changes occurring in the organization that I now lead. We wanted to position ourselves as an organization for effective mission in the twenty-first century. The result had been a time of major transition both in our structures and our attitudes. Change is never easy, and reframing an organization and refocusing good people who had been with us for years had made it all the more difficult.

Returning to my office, I found myself wondering why she felt the need to state this truth so emphatically. I had never seen myself as the kind of person who needs to change things for the sake of shaking things up. Neither did I see myself as the kind of leader who forced change on others.

There was no question that her statement was correct; change for change's sake is nothing more than "the tinkering of the bored." I have watched some church leaders "play with" and "create" change simply because they are bored or, even worse, spiritually stale. They needed change to wake themselves up, and consequently projected their needs on others.

G. K. Chesterton has a wonderful way of describing the effects of this kind of boredom. He writes: "There comes an hour in the afternoon when the child is tired of 'pretending,' when he is weary of being a robber or a cowboy. It is then when he torments the cat... The effect of this staleness is the same everywhere."[2]

Change that emerges out of boredom is dangerous. We are tired of pretending, so we torment the cat. Unfortunately, the "cat" can be the unsuspecting church members caught in the stale and dry spiritual life of their leaders.

Change for change's sake is never helpful. Staying the course is not helpful either, especially when all the signs tell us that it is a critical time to make course corrections. Skillful leaders nurture a sense of urgency in their congregations. They foster a passionate desire to see the church live out its intended purpose to sing the song in this new and strange world. This is the crucial difference between congregations that live in their memories and those who live in anticipation of the future.

Change as Deep Change

Change is never easy. We need to be reminded about this truth on a daily basis. It is the rare person in the church who does not realize that some kind of shift or change needs to take place. Intuitively we know that something different needs to happen in our desire to more effectively engage our culture with the gospel of Jesus Christ.

Most of us want change to be easy. If we are going to sing, let it be a familiar tune. It would be nice if change allowed things to be remarkably similar to the way they were before.

Others will embrace a new song, but only at "arm's length." They accept that alterations and shifts need take place in their congregations, but reserve the right to withdraw or say "I told you so" if the desired result does not happen. Amazingly, the "arm's length" parishioners are always right, because they never embrace or endorse anything without hedging their commitments enough to pull out if it doesn't work.

Still others feel a God-ordained right to save leaders from themselves. Their task it to make sure leaders do not get away with anything. This is particularly virulent in smaller churches where leaders are not given the opportunity to lead. These people see the role of congregational meetings as a "check up" time when the members come together to question everything the leader has done.

I heard of a situation in which the outgoing moderator of an elders' board took the incoming moderator out for lunch before he handed over the mantel of leadership. He told the new leader in deep sincerity that the job of moderator was to ensure that the minister not get away with anything. The new leader was shocked and approached the pastor to inquire if this was indeed his job description. The result was a wonderful time of prayer and discussion about leadership and the new moderator's leadership was defined over the next year by wise counsel and a liberating empowerment to pastoral staff and people in ministry at the church.

Whether you like it or not, the only control you have in change is your ability to deal with yourself. You can choose how you approach, embrace, and deal with transitions around you. Leaders who are facilitating change–*and* people who go through change–must first begin with themselves. Stephen Covey affirms this truth: the only person that you have direct and immediate control over is yourself.[3]

You have choices to make in the change process. Effective leaders wishing transformational change in their congregations must first be transformed. Whether it is strategic and focused change, or "change for change's sake" out of boredom and staleness, it begins with you. Cultural change starts with personal change.

Challenged by Two Worlds

My wife and I attend a small church near our home. When we moved into the city, we chose this church very quickly because we wanted to attend a congregation in our community so that we could be involved with people who live in our neighborhood. This small vibrant congregation of approximately 100 people is a multicultural mix of different language groups, socioeconomic backgrounds, faith backgrounds, and church experience. In many ways, we reflect the new fabric of Toronto. Ours is a city where the majority of the population is from somewhere else. The United Nations has declared that Toronto is the most multicultural urban area in the world. Effective churches in this city are slowly reflecting this new reality.

Our neighborhood church actually has a long history in the community. Once a blue-collar neighborhood surrounded by factories, the community has changed dramatically. It now consists of a mix of low-cost rental apartments for recent immigrants, luxury condos on the lakefront, old homes being gobbled up at high prices by young professionals who want a family-like neighborhood, and old residential housing where owners have lived for decades.

The people who make up the congregation are both the present and the future. There is a pocket of old residents, the faithful who stayed in the church and saw it through the difficult times in the past. They are trustees of the legacy of this church and stewards of its present. The new people represent an ethnic and spiritual mix. Many are exploring an intuitive desire to encounter God, but with little background and foundation from which they can draw.

Some have come from no Christian background whatsoever. Theirs is a journey with little negative baggage. All is new and therefore captivating in its freshness. Others are coming back, seeking a home where they can share their spiritual inquisitiveness, yet are wary of institutional religious life. They come with a genuine desire to find God while also anxious that their spiritual quest may not be respected.

Our congregation faces some interesting issues. Some are as easy as learning to move over as others move into our space. For a church that was declining for many years, new faces in the pews can be very encouraging. The challenge, however, is much more attitudinal and atmospheric. It will require theological reflection as well as relational skill. The tensions are palpable in our congregation. They are the tensions of singing the song in this strange land. The faithful want the song to be the same. Please understand, we do sing choruses. We even project the lyrics onto the wall. The problem is that the songs of language and rhythms, attitudes and acceptance are still sung from the old hymnbook.

Our pastor is constantly challenged by these two worlds. There is not a lot of animosity expressed, but well-meaning and loving people who are anxious about this foreign land in which they are living keep trying to lead us back into the old song.

It Isn't about You: It Is about God

"It isn't about you!" This is how Rick Warren starts his book *The Purpose Driven Life.*[4] It seems like an obvious truth, but it remains a constant struggle within the people of God. It is what defines a church in the borderland. The consumer nature of church in North America has not been useful in pressing home this point. Eddie Gibbs writes:

> This consumer-focused approach to ministry successfully attracted crowds, but it has failed for the most part to transform lives or construct the significant personal relationships that provide encouragement, spiritual growth, accountability and avenues for Christian ministry… More and more people spend their time just shopping around, looking for diversion while avoiding commitment.[5]

If most conflicts in the church were shaped around seeking what is best for God's purpose for the church, it would be amazing how the conversations would differ. We are part of a large purpose. God's desire is to announce his reign on earth through a people so passionately involved in this mission that they can do nothing less than become the people of God.

A REST STOP ALONG THE WAY

- Do you know of congregations that have become "shells of their past in size and influence"? Share what you know of their stories. Hold onto these stories and use them as case examples within which to discuss the ideas presented in this book.
- What are the changes that have taken place in church life in your area since 1955? What are the changes that have taken place in your neighborhood?

- In what ways do you relate to the experience of the psalmist's question, "How do I sing my song of faith here in this new world?" In what ways is your church asking, "How do we be the church in these strange times?"

2

Crossing Over

Discovering the Missional Nature of the Church

BORDERLAND COMPASS POINT

Joshua's experience of moving across the Jordan to the promised land serves as a framework for today's church to move from the security of our North American subculture to the borderlands. The Hebrew word *'abar,* "crossover," defines the experience of not being able to go back to the familiar nor being able to stay where we currently find ourselves. The church must step out into what is next if new possibilities of missional effectiveness and health are to be encountered. It must recapture the essence and centrality of its missional nature, the very nature of a sending God.

In the eighties, my family lived in a downtown neighborhood in the marvelous cultural mix of Toronto. This area was entering a time of renewal and reflected a wonderful mosaic of people. Young families were moving in to renovate old houses that had been home to families in previous generations. It was a neighborhood of vast differences and colorful characters.

One wonderful character was Tony. He had immigrated from Sicily forty years before with his wife and was now nearing retirement. He had raised his family and built a little bit of Italy in his backyard, where grapes hung on trestles. Each year he made his own wine and bottled it in large glass soda bottles. Every time we did some work to fix our yard or house, a bottle of his special concoction would appear at our door, an affirmation that we were participating in his great desire to clean up the neighborhood.

The neighborhood even had its own baseball team. It formed itself each spring and played through the summer twice a week. You could not have formed a more comical mix of people. A television news reporter from the national broadcasting network, a criminologist, a Jewish labor lawyer, and a Marxist sociology professor were just a few of the people who made up the team. We were invited because we had come to know a couple across the street over the winter and they vouched for us. It is an interesting principle–most people need someone in the neighborhood to vouch for you or you will never be accepted.

At the first practice we were given a grilling about everything from our playing ability (not too bad because Carla can hit it out of the park) to our schedules. They also wanted to know what we were doing as Western Canadians now living in this metropolitan city. It was one of those awkward moments. I had to tell them my occupation. In other places this often stops conversations for a moment. Our daughter was in elementary school. My wife was studying theology at the time and, while the topic was a bit odd, being a student was within the realm of acceptability. However, my career as a Baptist minister was *definitely* odd. I was their first. Luckily, our friends from across the street continued to vouch for us in the awkward moments of silence as they pondered my strangeness.

What happened over the following years was a profound realignment of my thinking about ministry and faithful living. We grew in friendships that gave rich input into our lives. The whole journey together was for only three years, yet each year was a progressive movement in relational depth.

The first year was exploratory. They learned about us. We were invited to the after parties, where we learned about family and issues at work. There, in those times of informal conversation, genuine and transparent friendships were made.

The second and third years brought a place of deepening comfort. Having finally confirmed my status as "normal," they found freedom to humorously discuss the relative merits of taking religion seriously and the remarkable odd fact that I was a minister. The latter was often brought up in introductions. They often announced with great pride, "He is a Baptist minister." I became their religious mascot and chaplain.

The humor often extended to the ball field, where I was even allowed to make fun of their lack of faith commitment. "Gary, God is watching," screamed our third base coach at a difficult moment in the final inning of a key game as I came to bat. "Oh, good," I tentatively replied, stepping out of the batter's box. "I thought I was like all of the rest of you–all alone." Don's face took on an amusing smirk, and he quickly retorted, "Yes, Gary, you are the lucky one." We had graduated into genuine community and were now part of the neighborhood, a place where giving and taking was comfortably offered.

The decision to leave Toronto for a call to pastoral ministry in Western Canada occurred during our third year of baseball. Not wanting to miss our final season, we stayed put for most of the summer. The day before we left, our teammates threw a BBQ backyard party to say their farewells. It was a great time of conversation, tastes, and laughter. Mostly, it was an emotional time of saying goodbye to people we had come to care for deeply.

At one point in the party, the conversations paused and Bob, the Marxist sociology professor from the local university, spoke for the group. He said that the group had been talking over the last couple of years about us. He admitted that they were at first taken back by our faith commitment and even more so of my being a minister of the Baptist persuasion, which, he noted, was not a plus for me. Over the last few years that we had played and laughed together, they as a group had gotten more intrigued by us. They wanted to ask us a question, a question that still fascinates me, "Do you fit?"

At first, we were both surprised by the question. Obviously they, like so many others, had "drawn caricatures" of who we are as people of faith. Those assumptions and presuppositions are usually as off the mark as those same generalizations we hold for people in the borderlands, those of other faiths or no faith. The reason for this is simple. Our friends were saying that their experience of us did not fit their prejudice about "our kind" of people.

What followed was an amazing time of conversation around our faith and our lives. Real things were said about our passions and our sense of call to what we both were doing. Mostly, it was a time of transparent and honest connection that we have never forgotten.

What would happen if we all just crossed over? This is the crucial question we face as people of faith on this side of the borderlands.

Would we be any worse for doing it? Is it really that strange a place, or is it a place we live in all the time but simply do not take that seriously or intentionally?

We may have forgotten that true understanding will only come through incarnational living among borderland people. Our observations provide labeling aids to church leaders desperately trying to grasp the challenges faced in the changing face of society. The words and descriptions quickly enter the vocabulary of pastors and leaders, becoming passwords for initiation into the club of relevance and pastoral competence.

We need to embrace a different way of knowing, one that moves us from description to an experience. Being able to put words to observations made by others is not enough. The greatest challenge is to move from theory and the broad generalities of descriptive writings to lived experience.

Crossing Over

The book of Joshua provides a helpful framework for this lived journey. It is captured in a Hebrew word that occurs for the first time in Joshua 3. The people of God are musing over their movement across the Jordan to the promised land. They are curious and afraid all at once as they gaze across the great river. Joshua, attempting to encourage and challenge them about their next step, speaks out. His words portray great understanding of the mix of emotions they are feeling as they look out into the unknown. He even heightens their anxiety, reminding them that they "have not passed this way before" (Josh. 3:4).

The only people who like change are usually the ones who are in charge of it. I am convinced that clergy do not totally grasp this truth. We think it is rational and reasonable to embrace change.

It is much better to appreciate the fact that, if we have not been this way before, our people will have a great degree of anxiety. We may have much to learn from the past regarding the challenges ahead, but "we have not been this way before." Leaders have more control in the changes ahead than their people.

Joshua seems to appreciate this. In speaking to the people, he chooses to use a Hebrew word to capture all they are experiencing at that moment. The word is *'abar* (pronounced HABAR) and it translates in the English text of scripture as "crossover." It becomes the watershed word that captures all they are experiencing.

They had spent forty years wandering in the desolate and barren wilderness. Their seemingly aimless meandering had become familiar to them. In truth, it had all become comfortable to them, eliciting a sense of safety in the reoccurring sameness. Human beings have a wonderful ability to adapt to what is strange and even uncomfortable.

So the writer of Joshua chooses words carefully. In fact, he chooses a word that is not used in the Old Testament until this moment, a word that captures everything the people are feeling and seeing. The word *'abar* (crossover) is used first in 3:1 and then over twenty-one times from chapter three to the middle of chapter five.

The meaning of the word emphasizes the decisive nature of the event. John Hamlin, in his book *Inheriting the Land*, makes this point. The word *'abar,* he says, has a decisive quality to it. It captures the finality required to cross over a boundary.[1] The people of God are about to cut themselves off from what has been their world, a world that was predictable. Something vastly different is about to take place. If taken, this crossover will place them in a position from which they will be unable to turn back.

You have probably lived an *'abar* moment at some point in your life. Sometimes you have willingly sought an *'abar* time. Some *'abar* times have been thrust on you. You may even be facing a personal *'abar* now. These frightening crossover moments are times of standing fearfully at the edge of your "Jordan" with the knowledge that the issues and experiences ahead are unknown.

At these times, you desperately want to hold onto the familiar. It is honest to realize that when you enter an *'abar* time, your life will forever be altered and you will never be able to return. You will never be the same again.

Living as the Church in the Crossover Time

Joshua speaks with odd but comforting words, providing a pictorial symbol of God. The Ark of the Covenant will be sent out in front of the people (Josh. 3:3-4.) It will be set down in the middle of the Jordan, pointing the way to the other side. It is meant to be a comforting presence. God will go out before us and God's presence will also be in the midst of our experience.

Undoubtedly, we are facing an *'abar* (crossover) time in the life of our church in North America. Numerous writings describe the times in which we find ourselves, but crossovers are experienced long before they are understood. Giving words to the experience is comforting, but the depth of the changes shaping us can never be captured in words. Our anxieties and fears are not caused by the inability to put our experience into words, as helpful as this is. They are a result of the experience and of our desire to cling to the familiar. The people of Israel felt similar emotions as they gazed across the Jordan.

"Crossing over" is rarely embraced willingly. It is, however, only in the crossing over that God's new thing becomes possible. Crossing over provides, as one management expert calls it, an opportunity for a "whack on the side of the head"[2] that will unlock us from thinking and living in the old familiar ruts.

Joshua presents the *'abar* process to the people of Israel. He also provides a helpful framework for our own crossovers by capturing the immediacy of the Israelites' experience with all of the emotion and mystery it holds for the future. He realizes that the only comforting thought he can offer is that God goes before and with them.

Stepping out into the Unknown

In *'abar* moments we realize that we cannot go back and neither can we stay where we are. There is inevitability to this moment. It reminds us that the first part of the journey always has an ending point. Rarely do we choose the endings in our lives. Usually, ending points are not predetermined. They just happen. The worst times are when they are imposed on us.

This may describe the feeling of many in the North American church of the twenty-first century. We did not ask for this world of unrest, religious wars, and continental conflicts. Fear grips us and the marginalization of the church in the midst of the uncertainty only accentuates our uneasiness. If God has brought us to this point, our powerlessness makes us want to resist change or, worse, simply play out our lives in subcultures of insignificant religious activity. In truth, we either embrace this crossover placed before us or sulk about what has been taken away.

I watched a group of people bungee jumping at a large indoor playground one day, and it caused me to reflect about critical points in *'abar.* People approached the edge of the platform and pondered the implications of stepping out into the unknown. There was a critical moment when many of the jumpers pondered the choice of stepping off, and many decided not to jump. Obviously, the most difficult time a person encountered was at the very point of decision. All the rest was taken care of by gravity and the rubber rope. You could feel the bungee jumper's angst and then I thought, "What would happen if someone just pushed him off? What if there was no choice?"

Crossover times imply moments of decision, but they are not always decisions we control. They are more often decisions of response. Choices also take place when we are simply pushed off the edge. In those times, we have to decide whether or not we will fight against the experience.

The church faces a similar decision: to lean into the experience or resist it. Like the people at the edge of the Jordan, churches might desire to look back or they may be willing to go out into the adventure of *'abar.* Wherever they are in that process, they must step out if new possibilities of missional effectiveness are to be explored.

Living in the In-Between Times

Strangely enough, the critical point has probably already taken place. We did not get a chance to make a choice. It just happened. Describing the changes taking place will not make the experience any easier. Mike Regele describes this phenomenon this way:

> Change today bears two characteristics that make it more unsettling than social change of the recent past. First, it is global rather than local. In the past, social change happened in larger or smaller regional pockets. If you really wanted to escape it, you could always move! Today's social change occurs on a global scale. It is inescapable.
>
> Second, the rate of social change moves at supersonic speed compared to the rate of change in the past. We have less and less time to reflect on the changes occurring around us. This is a luxury of the past. Any organization or institution that continues to behave as if we had all the time in the world to reflectively consider the full implications of modern change will be trampled by change and will cease to exist.[3]

Churches are discovering this. They know they are in this "in-between time" of a crossover. Rapid changes within the societal and global landscape impact everything churches do. The irony is, while living in this in-between time, they often live with the delusion that they still have a decision to make about engaging this new world. They have been pushed off the bank a long time ago and still do not realize it. The choice was made for them. Their only decision now is how they engage change.

The in-between time is a strange place. It is neither the beginning nor the end. It is just a place of transition. Some prefer to think that we are on the other side. They love to describe this time as if it is a finished place. They give it labels to popularize it but it feels exactly as it sounds: in-between with no end in sight.

Here choices are crucial. We either accept the reality of the place we find ourselves in or pretend it has not occurred. The option to go back really does not exist except in ever-vanishing pockets of subcultured society. Learning the new songs and rhythms of this time will be difficult if we ignore the altered landscape we are in. It will be equally difficult to accept new information to inform our present if we will only listen to what we once heard.

The issue is not change; it is facing realities and deciding how to engage them. There is, however, a time of listening and reflecting that is critical. Choosing to see this crossover as a problem to be solved and working to bring it to premature solutions may cause you to pitch your tent in the middle of the Jordan. The results could be catastrophic. This is a time to allow God to reshape and to reveal the questions required to challenge the faulty presuppositions that have been held about church. This is not a time to survive or a problem to solve. It is a time for God to make something new.

During these moments of desiring to impossibly return to what we know, we also may want to dash across to the other side. When that desire overtakes us, it is usually due to the mistaken idea that the goal is the other side and not the journey. That is when we believe that the in-between is to be endured and the other side is the prize. When we think like this we can prematurely assume that we have reached the other bank. Hurriedly, we pitch our tents, ignoring the unresolved issues that could have only been dealt with while on the journey.

The Ark of the Covenant goes before the people of Israel and is set up in the middle of the Jordan for a reason. It is meant to stand as a reassuring presence to the people caught in the midst of the most difficult part of *'abar*. The Ark represents the presence of God in their lives. It is there to secure and ground the people, so they do not run out ahead and miss what is to be learned through God's work in them.

We have an innate belief that these times, not unlike the biblical concept of "wilderness," are times when problems must be fixed. However, many assumed them to be bumps on the road rather than part of the journey of our faith.

This is likely why we move so quickly to solutions. We are uncomfortable with the ambiguity and uncertainty these times bring. They have a way of causing us to question and challenge our presuppositions. We believe that comfort will only come from resolving the problems. And, we believe, the faster the better.

I remember a conversation with a group of very effective clergy in my own country, many from very large churches. They were being challenged to look at congregational life in a new way, and all of them admitted to a frustrating intuitive feeling that growing a bigger and better church was not creating more effective disciples. Neither were they convinced that their highly effective "come to" congregations were incarnationally engaging with the communities around them. They were experiencing the in-between nature of *'abar* and it was discomforting. Rather than questioning their understanding of the church and its mission, however, the conversation quickly moved to the places in which they were more comfortable: the "how to" of fixing their problems.

When we see these times as problem-solving times and move too hurriedly to resolve, we miss God's solutions. If we do that, we miss the deeper questions that must be asked. These questions make us uncomfortable because they dig at the roots of our faith and our convictions about church. This may be the reason many people feel uneasy about the conversations taking place under the umbrella of the emerging church movement. These Christian leaders are raising fundamental questions about how we do church by pointing to things we may not desire to see.

This time in the life of the North American church needs to be seen in different ways. The issues we are facing are a wonderful opportunity to discover what God wants to shape in us. Resting in the part of the journey and seeking to live totally engaged in this "not yet" experience will be crucial to what emerges as the church in the future.

A Time of New Beginnings

I must confess to be unwilling to write on this topic at this point. In many ways, it is not worth discussing because most of it would be conjecture. We are at best in the in-between times. Although many writers would like to point to a possible future, it is not yet present. What it means to be the church in this time is unfolding and it is helpful, both from a faith and a congregational perspective, for us to dwell in that uncertainty for a time.

I also must confess to some cynicism and deep concern about triumphantly confident assertions by some current leaders that their model of worship, gathering or scattering, is the new beginning.

I prefer to live in the journey of what might unfold so that what is possible might be actualized. Joshua reminds us that we "have not been this way before" and we do well to recover the humble sensitivity required to live in this unknown time. By doing so, we will protect ourselves from moving too quickly to shallow cosmetic solutions rather than to the deeper adjustments required for effectively living in this time as the church.

So What?

This is a fair question. Please endure one more Canadian moment. It seems to me that people south of our border are often very quick in their movement to solutions. This is not a political comment, although it could be explored from that perspective. It is an observation about a trait in the American psyche that is both admirable and simplistic. It produces that amazing entrepreneurial spirit that allows Americans to act in the profound belief that there is not a problem or issue without a solution.

The shadow side can be dangerous and destructive. It periodically instills movement toward easy fixes and quick solutions because it has not paused long enough in reflection and listening. The successes and failures of such an approach to problem solving are evident around the world.

Canadians, on the other hand, are frozen in analysis. We can see the problems and diligently examine all sides and surfaces while unconsciously attempting not to act at all. It sometimes evokes in us a sense of moral superiority. We are not running to solutions, nor looking for the quick fixes, so we should be admired for our angst and struggle. Neither are we moving deeper or, for that matter, moving at all.

I have realized that the person who doggedly examines and analyzes is not unlike the hurried problem solver. We find comfort in the fact that we are at least doing something. Canadians just do it in our heads. Americans act; we simply think.

Jonathan Wilson captures these two poles and provides a helpful alternative. He writes:

> Those same extremes are present in the church when we think, on the one hand, that marketing techniques and management skills will lead to effectiveness, success and growth. Or when we fall into the error, on the other hand, of thinking that we have no contribution to make, therefore we are entirely passive. The correction to these errors is not some synthesis or middle way but a third way of thinking about the church. In this third way, we become participants in God's work by God's grace.[4]

The Journey toward Transformation

It is here, when we step away from the things that we once knew and move toward the unknown, that life, mission, and congregational renewal take place. Renewal will not emerge from new programs, transformed denominational structures, or creative strategies. This *'abar* time will require a reframing of attitudes, assumptions, and frameworks long before the finished product emerges. You will need a new mind-set that will only emerge from a people willing to step out into a place that they have never been before, willing to journey more deeply with God in this time.

This is the place where we discover, or rediscover, a God who is present and at work. Joshua 3:10 says it this way, "By this you shall know that among you is the living God." It is here where God surprises us: "tomorrow the LORD will do wonders among you" (Josh. 3:5). Effective borderland living comes from the kind of people who are open to the God who is the ever-present surprise of the Christian life and sovereign over the church and its mission.

Some Discoveries on the Journey

One of the many things that we as the church in North America are learning in this *'abar* experience is that we are living in mission fields in which more and more people have less and less Christian memory. Darrell Guder points out:

> The Christian church (in Canada and the US) finds itself in a very different place in relation to its context. Rather than occupying a central and influential place, [Canadian and US] Christian churches are increasingly marginalized, so much so that in our urban areas they represent a minority movement. It is by now a truism to speak of North America as a mission field.[5]

It does not matter whether you are talking about Australia, New Zealand, or Western Europe, the landscape has drastically altered.

We have spent years sending missionaries around the world, but now *we* are mission fields. Having done missions "over there," we are still captive to the mind-set that mission only happens "over there." Too often the people in authority and leadership still work from the "over there" mind-set. This enables them to believe that they can continue to do things the way they have always been done or, worse, simply make some superficial changes.

Crossing over into the Missional Nature of the Church

The French have a saying, "Plus que change, plus c'est la même" (translation: "The more things change, the more it remains the same"). It is possible that this journey is similar to journeys taken by the church in other times. Leaders and catalysts for transformation in those times asked questions about their times and reflected on what might make the church vibrant, alive, and relevant. They were asking the question that every generation must ask, "What does it mean to be the church in this time?" This crucial question must be asked, regardless of the resistance, because it rises from the desire to be effective missionaries.

Some things, however, never change. They are the constants that stand as the core nonnegotiables required to live out the gospel. One of those nonnegotiables is this understanding of the missional nature of the church. Guder addresses this nonnegotiable missional nature of the church through his understanding of the "mission of God." He writes:

> Mission means "sending," and it is the central biblical theme describing the purpose of God's action in human history. God's mission began with the call of Israel to receive God's blessings in order to be a blessing to the nations. God's mission unfolded in the history of God's people across the centuries recorded in Scripture, and it reached its revelatory climax in the incarnation of God's work of salvation in Jesus ministering, crucified and resurrected. God's mission continued then in the sending of the Spirit to call forth and empower the church as the witness to God's good news in Jesus Christ. It continues today in the worldwide witness of churches in every culture to the gospel of Jesus Christ, and it moves toward the promised consummation of God's salvation in the eschaton ("last" or "final day").[6]

The church that is emerging in this crossover time is very different from the churches that grew out of the last two decades of the twentieth century.

Many churches, while actively seeking to be sensitive to others in the community, continued to operate in the old "come to" model of church life. Contemporary writers often call it the attractional model.[7] This attractional model is really a product of Christendom, in which Christianity was a dominant frame in society. It is also the model that the modern missionary movement cloned around the world. In some African countries, for example, this has come to be known as the "compound model," in which the church invites the community to come to the compound where needs will be met: water, health clinics, and worship–all at the same place. While the motivation is commendable, the result is too often a fortress mentality. If people come, they will be served.

New styles of worship in the last twenty years intentionally worked to attract people who liked the new way of being church.

Evangelism was the way to encourage nonattenders to join them, and the way of doing church was "ramped up" without necessarily altering the underlying approach. It still was framed under the idea that if we get a group of Christians together and express church in a way that we enjoy and invite others to come along, we will grow because people will come.

Many of these churches met with considerable success. Sometimes they were accused of attracting Christians from other churches who might have been leaving congregations that no longer scratched them where they itched. However, they also appealed to lapsed Christians and people with some Christian background who were entering a new spiritual journey.

The profound shift taking place in this crossover time is much deeper and radical. The shift is toward intentionally taking the church into the world, replacing the "you come to us" framework with a "we'll come to you" approach.

The inadequacy of the "come to" framework is painfully obvious. Eddie Gibbs and Ryan Bolger describe it this way:

> When Christians focus on a "come structure" for church, they cease to be missional in that they are asking those outside the Christian faith to come into their world instead of serving in the world of those outside. As shown by Jesus and his interaction with the temple authorities, the kingdom typically lies outside existing religious structures. Christians need to find God "out there."[8]

Steve Collins of Grace Church in London, England, gives further content to this inadequacy when he says, "people would no more drop into a church for a casual visit than an outsider might drop into a mosque or a gay bar for a casual visit. One wouldn't quite know how to behave and may wonder what other people think."[9]

Journeying away from Tinkering and Reworking

This crossover time is creating communities of faith that are absolutely committed to defining the church and its effectiveness not by what is taking place inside the walls of the church but by what is happening outside. Effectiveness is measured by the ways in which their church members effectively engage the borderland people of their networks and neighborhoods. Leonard Sweet told a group of students and faculty that we are in midst of a "perfect storm." He said, "Christians in the West can no longer expect to have that home-court advantage... God is defragging and rebooting the church."[10]

Sweet points out in much of his writings that old models are killing the church in the West. He says, "out-dated models of church that are 'attractional, propositional and colonial' are being replaced by models that are 'missional, relational and incarnational.'"[11]

This rediscovery of our missional mandate as the church creates possibilities for the difficult work of shaping ministry to a particular context. The only foundational hope for purposeful engagement of the borderlands dweller is the appearance of a visible and faithfully engaged church in the life of its communities and neighborhoods. When that occurs, the church becomes a unique and distinct missional presence.

Making the Missional Church Framework Accessible

The writings of Lesslie Newbigin have become the foundational content of much of what we now call the missional church movement.[12] Newbigin was a bishop in the Methodist church in India. When he returned to England after years of missionary service, he discovered to his surprise that England had become a mission field. His observations are an indictment on the church, not just in the UK, but also in North America as he calls us to transcend our passive attractional models of being the church.

Newbigin noted that it was not enough to understand culture and then shape your mission and ministry to it; you must first be shaped by the gospel. You must ask what it means to be a gospel community in your own culture and context. He called this the "heretical imperative," standing in the midst of the community and saying, "We are for you but you need to know that our values are shaped by the Gospel." This call to reimagine the church as a force in the community rather than as a place shaped to receive borderland people if they choose to come is a distinct paradigm shift for many average churchgoers.

You cannot underestimate how difficult that reimaging can be. Crossing over in mind-set and activity is a direct assault on the way that we have traditionally done church. It confronts the majority of things that we do because it invites us to move from words that we speak about outreach and the activities that are singularly unconnected to the way that we do everything else in the church. In doing so, they invite us to focus our energy out into the community.

A congregation I am familiar with meets directly across from a high school and yet for years never saw its mission field as that place. That does not mean that they did not discuss outreach to it. The fact that it was always a place for outreach was obvious, but to treat it as a mission field was different than treating it as an outreach point. Occasionally they invited the students to join in something that they were doing, but they failed to enter into the rhythms, concerns, and faces of that place. The result was a strange detachment.

Finally, they imagined another way of being the church to the school. They introduced themselves to the administration in the desire to be an incarnational presence in the place. They asked questions about what struggles the students, teachers, and administrators face. They even went so far as to add to the dialogue their own concerns. As part of their conversations and emerging new relationship, they asked how they could join with the school in their journey of shaping and educating students toward productive citizenship. They even sought to understand what activities and programs the school genuinely needed.

In this borderland missional journey, the church is learning about the incarnational energy that enabled the early church to turn its world upside down. In its emergent beginnings, the early church believed that knowing Christ also meant taking on the *missio dei,* the redemptive mission of God to the whole world. To firmly grasp God's mission was to see it in the light of Jesus. He came to announce and demonstrate the coming of the kingdom of God and its presence now. He wanted us to know that under God's reign in Christ the whole world is being redeemed and the church is the sign of that possibility: a taste of the presence of the kingdom.

In the first centuries, *missio dei* was assumed in the Trinitarian nature of the church. It was captured in the understanding of the nature of God who, because of his seeking and sending nature, sends the Son to the world. The Son then gifts the church in its birth at Pentecost with the Spirit. This Spirit empowered the early church in such a way that its first inclination is not to form committees and constitutions but instead to fling itself into the world in gospel ministry of word and deed. The hope of the gospel in the New Testament was a church that lived this out.

One of Newbigin's contemporaries, David Bosch, elaborated on this sending quality of God's trinitarian being:

> Mission [is] understood as being derived from the very nature of God. It [is] thus put in the context of the doctrine of the trinity, not of ecclesiology (theology of the church) or soteriology (the theology of salvation). The classical doctrine of *missio Dei* as God the Father sending the Son, and God the Father and the Son sending the Spirit [is] expanded to

include yet another "movement": Father, Son and Holy Spirit sending the church into the world.[13]

The *missio dei* emerges from the very nature of who God is. It takes place long before the church is formed and it implicates everything we do. As we reimagine the church in our crossover to the borderlands, we do so in the profound belief that we are not taking God there; God is already there. Our task is to find out where God is at work and to join God's activity. Ryan Bolger and Eddie Gibbs give great perspective on this when they write: "The *missio dei* changes the functional direction of church…from a centrifugal (flowing in) to a centripetal (flowing out) dynamic. This in turn [leads] to a shift in emphasis from attracting crowds to equipping, dispersing and multiplying Christ followers as a central function of the church."[14]

How Will We Know We Are Crossing Over?

It is really quite easy to tell if you are crossing over. Borderland churches begin to express themselves in mood and atmosphere long before they move to programs. It begins with a new attitude that can only be described as "openness"–an openness expressed in the way they embrace God's ideas and surprises. The creativity expressed by a borderland church manifests itself when the church does not shut down new ideas or strategies. Instead, members ask the exploratory question, "Why not?"

Leadership in borderland churches reflects an understanding of the church existing for others. Decisions, as a result, are made according to that principle. I still remember when a great saint of our congregation came to report the defacing of a white couch in the women's lounge area. It seems that two young expressive boys decided to write their names in broad strokes on the back of the couch with a felt marker. I had spotted the crime a few days earlier and anticipated the anger it might elicit. I had been somewhat apprehensive and I attempted to hide the evidence by pushing the couch up against the wall. To my surprise, this dear saint was not angry. She only had come to tell me what had happened and that she had cleaned it off. As she left my office, she said, "Gary, I can remember when there were no children here. I will put up with some mess."

Borderland churches know their neighbors, their politicians, and their neighboring businesses. They share in the community activities and are recognized by the agencies that work there. They are a presence not just through their buildings but through their social networks.

Our daughter and son-in-law go to an amazing church in their northern Alberta town. Theirs is a church of approximately 120 people and they continue to move out into the neighborhood by creating programs that are not simply designed for their own people but for the community. The have even developed one of those "out of the box" ideas that emerge when people are open to anything. It is an outreach event on Sunday morning called "Breakfast Church." People bring friends for breakfast, a kind of brunch worship experience.

I realize that this may appear to be very "come to" in its frame. Understand, however, that many people in congregations are so busy in their church activities that they do not have the time to develop relationships with people in the borderlands. The beauty of this vibrant small church is that they do. Their friends know that they will be part of a short worship service with a faith exploration message, but they come because of the incarnational relationships that have been developed with people from the church.

On one occasion, I spoke at this event. It was delightful to see the enjoyment and the way in which this little church went about making things comfortable for their visitors. More than half of the people in attendance were from the unfaithed and unconnected church frame. They were borderland people. It was a delightful time as we talked about "Life after Breakfast" at this incredible event. The church on regular Sundays represents the messy diversity of this oil and chemical refinery town. The great majority of the congregation was not attending church until they arrived in this place.

Serving a Missionary God

Samuel Escobar captures the missional intention of God's purpose when he says, "The mission to which God sends those he chooses is always a 'mission impossible' possible only because God will act in order to accomplish his purposes."[15] We would do well to remember this. Life in the borderlands is simply an act of obedience to that which we have been called to do as part of our discipleship to Jesus Christ.

Crossing over into the borderlands should not be seen as the latest program designed to make the church effective in these times. It is simply living out God's commission as to what we should do and be: God's people in the world of neighborhoods and networks. This is God's gift of missional focus to us. Churches responding to this gift cross over into the borderlands because they have asked the crucial question of borderland living, "Why has God placed us, a community of faith, at this time in this neighborhood and in this context?" In doing so, they find God in the most surprising places.

A REST STOP ALONG THE WAY

- Recall and share some of your "crossing over" stories, stories in which you have had experiences with borderland people. Discuss what it was that made you feel uncomfortable in this strange place and what helped you to see your world in a different way.
- Take the time to study chapters 3–5 in the book of Joshua, paying particular attention to the words and phrases referring to crossing over. Identify the experience of *'abar* in your own life. How close to an *'abar* time is your church?
- Of what significance is it that the Ark of the Covenant is in the midst of and is out ahead of the people of God?
- Do you agree with the suggestion that we too often move to solutions and may be bypassing a critical step in the journey if we move too quickly out of the in-between time? Give an example from your church life.
- What might it mean for your church "to be a gospel community in your own culture and context"?

3

Recovering Our Roots

God's Intent for His Church

BORDERLAND COMPASS POINT

Using the church at Ephesus as a case study, today's churches are being invited into a process of rediscovery. This process calls us to re-examine our theology of our image of the church. It also calls us to reexamine our hope for the church in order to recapture God's intention: the called out, called together, called for, and called to nature of the church. It is this intent that gives substance to the church as a borderland community.

I have always been intrigued when people express a desire to be more like the New Testament Church. It causes me to wonder which of the messy and imperfect early churches they want to emulate. All of them were living, breathing human communities not unlike the ones we attend. So what is it about those churches that people today desire? More importantly, do they know what they are asking for?

The greatest secret of the Christian faith is the community of the local church. At its best there is nothing like it on the face of the earth. But this "best" may be something much deeper, more radical and revolutionary than many of us may want. To be the church that God intended may mean a fundamental rediscovery of what it means to be the church of Jesus Christ. This "best" is God's intent established into and through a community of frail people. Surprisingly, God placed his mission in the heart of community living. He called the church to be a peculiar people set apart for the mission of fleshing out a taste of what might be in the world if God's reign of justice and righteousness were a reality. This is what God did. We need to recapture why God did it.

An Ephesian Case Study

God's intention for the church can be understood through an examination of the life of the church in Ephesus. Luke describes its beginnings in his early history of the church. He records that through Paul the small body of believers was birthed in this thriving metropolis (Acts 19:1–9). Later in the New Testament, Paul's letters to the Ephesians and to Timothy give us a picture of its formation as a community and its incorporation of missional purposes. A final snapshot of the Ephesian church, as recorded in Revelations, sadly reveals a church that has lost its reason for being.

Writing to the Ephesians, Paul sets out a foundational way of thinking about the church. It is grounded in a way of understanding why the community existed and in the implications those foundational beliefs had in their life together. This was not a theoretical dialogue. Paul wrote during a time of great struggle for the church, and he wanted them to know what it would mean to be the church during their time. While his main theme is unity, he develops a full and complete view of what we now call a theology of the church, captured by principles concerning our life together as a community of faith and the overriding missional purpose we have as God's peculiar people.

The challenge for leaders to form missional church life is daunting. The fledgling Ephesian church was not particularly easy to lead. This is vividly portrayed as Paul writes to Timothy, who was serving as the pastoral leader of the volatile congregation at the time. Timothy's frustration with these difficult people brought him to the brink of quitting and leaving that church for good. It appears that Paul is writing to challenge him to hang in with them.

The book of Revelation pictures the church's decline as it loses its passionate purpose (Rev. 2:1–6). It had turned in on itself. From the earliest inception of the church, they were an engaged people, living out the kingdom values of faith. They had turned the city of Ephesus on its economic head by being a distinct and purposeful people in their life together and in their personal virtue. This had threatened both the corruptive religious and political practices within the city. At the same time, this vibrant church had provided a place that freed others from the bondage of superstitions and unjust systems that were the foundation of urban life in Ephesus.

So what went wrong at the church? Why do the words of God spoken through John's Revelation appear to be so harsh to a people that could be commended for their commitment to the church, the hard work undertaken to keep the church afloat, devotion to the faith, and their willingness even to suffer persecution? Why are those things not enough to please God?

The words are harsh, but the answer appears to boil down to one thing: they "abandoned the love [they] had at first" (Rev. 2:4). In my words, they lost their passion. People who live in the passionate purpose of their first love will risk anything and do anything for what they believe. Nothing is too much and nothing is too inconvenient. When we lose that passionate love, however, we also lose the radical purpose of our existence.

I have been in numerous churches similar to the Ephesian congregation, in which faithful orthodox people still cling to programs and ministries that they have kept going with deep commitment. But something is missing. Invariably the missing something is captured in the same few words–they have lost their passionate purpose. All that is left is a desire to survive.

In the movie *The Guardian,* Kevin Costner plays a crusty old petty officer who is one of the best rescue divers in the U.S. Coast Guard. Through a series of events, he comes to be a teacher at the school where he learned his craft and, as is typical to these plots, encounters a younger brash diver. There comes a point in the movie where something new has taken place in both the lives of the teacher and the students. The officer walks onto the poolside and, with his back to the students, asks this question, "If I am lost, will you come find me?" The students respond with confident assurance, "Yes, petty officer, if you are lost, we will come find you?" He then asks a second question, "If I am drowning, will you come save me?" Again they reply, "Yes petty officer, if you are drowning, we will come save you." At that moment there is a poignant pause that culminates with the petty officer turning to the students and speaking these words, "I believe you would." A question haunts me: Will our love for God drive us into a world where people are lost and drowning? I wonder what answer God will give to us. I long to hear, "I believe you would."

John's revelation depicts a people who once felt deeply about God's purpose and now those feelings are foreign. The "first love" once had been the catalyst for everything they did, but somehow it disappeared, replaced with safe, unrisky, and internally focused institutional community life. I have visited many congregations entrenched in this Ephesian-like lostness.

Recovering a Theology of the Church

What you believe about the church has a direct impact on who you think belongs to the church, on how you live alongside one another, and how you minister. These beliefs shape what you celebrate as successful and effective and even how you evaluate personal faith.

Consider replacing the word *theology* with the word *image.* Just as every church has an implicit theology, it also exudes a dominant image of itself. Sometimes, the image may be one that was formed at a particular time in history. For other churches, the image may have developed through several experiences. Unfortunately, the image we hold may in fact have little to do with God's intention for the church. It may have more to do with a dominant narrative that has been perpetuated over the years.

It is helpful to realize that the New Testament does not start with a treatise on what the church should be. It begins with the church as a reality. It was a happening in history before it found content around its purpose. It was only later, as people struggled to understand what they were trying to become, that what we now call a theology of the church was articulated, largely through Paul's writings.

The church is at the heart of the New Testament story, just as it continues to be the heart of God's redemptive activity in the world. God's reconciling activity in Jesus Christ (2 Cor. 5:19) has as its goal not only the creation of individual holiness (Rom. 5:10–11) and a redeemed creation (Col. 1:20), but also, in the creation of community, a reconciliation between one another (Eph. 2:14–22).

The church as it existed in New Testament times is only a means to an end whereby the reign of God is made possible even in the smallest, most imperfect, way. Missiologists have spoken of the church as the only part of God's kingdom with a consciousness of the kingdom and therefore a responsibility for its preservation, celebration, and extension.

We live with the same problem today. The church is a reality. The challenge is to recapture God's intention at the time of its inception. We get sidetracked into focusing on the activity of the church rather than its purpose. We have chosen to look more at models that would be helpful for its success and growth without seeking to search deeper into what it must become. Recapturing this profound and ancient view of the church and its role in the reign of God is the critical foundational activity for today's expression of the church.

In order to articulate our theology of the church, or to evaluate the wholesomeness of our dominant image, we need to go back to the basics: the who, what, how, and why of God's intended purpose.

"Called Out" Who ...is this community of God's intent?	"Called Together" What ...is this community like?	"Called For" How ...will this community function?	"Called To" Why ...does the community exist?
Eph. 1:3-10; 3:3-6	Eph.1:7-8; 2:1,9,11-22	Eph. 1:13; 2:5,18	Eph. 1:6,18; 2:8-10; 3:18-19; 4:11-16
We who have been called out of the world by God	To be a new community of reconciliation and social healing	By being in relationship to Him and by Him	Because we are on a mission
We who have been set apart in much the same way as the people of God in the Old Testament	To not just live as individuals but as a community belonging to God and embodying His concerns	By allowing God to be at the heart of our community call to be together	Because we are on the move
We who live in the knowledge of who brought us out	To be a place to belong, to find grace and forgiveness and to demonstrate a new way of living together	By understanding that there is no other reason that we are together (1 Peter 1:23-2:4)	Because we are to be God's presence on Earth
We who are a people, holy and dearly loved	To be Priesthood for all	By becoming friends with God	Because as the Body of Christ we are His continuing presence incarnationally
Quality of our Sense of Identity and Purpose	**Quality of Relationship to Each Other in the Church**	**Quality of Relationship to Christ**	**Quality of Relationship to the World**

"Called Out": Who Is This Community of God's Intent?

In my seminary days at Fuller, professor Robert Munger drew a very simple diagram on the chalkboard to describe the people of God as ones whose entire direction in life has been completely altered by their commitment to Jesus Christ. He referred to it as the "upside-down nature of God's new creation." It illustrates the profound sense in which most of the world lives out the drama of a life–a constant power exchange and struggle to get to the top. The upside-down kingdom is a place where the last are first, the least are important, and to find life you must lose it. These are the dissenting themes of the new creation God has established. These themes point to a better way. The call to servanthood is the nonconformist thread that characterizes life in Christ. It is an inevitable and necessary expression of the church's nature.

From the beginning, God's redemptive plan was putting first an individual (Abraham), then a tribe and nation (the Israelites), and finally a people (the church) who would be set apart to be God's new society. This people of God, called a "holy nation" and "royal priesthood" in 1 Peter 2:9–10, are particularly odd because they represent a profoundly different way of living life together as a community, while at the same time existing for others. Jimmy Long writes, "The mission of the church since the time of Christ is to embody this reconciled community and invite others to be reconciled and renewed by joining this community."[1] Paul picks up this important theme in Ephesians. He says God's purpose was "to create in himself one new humanity in place of the two, thus making peace" (Eph. 2:15). These writers called on the church to be something different and distinct, both essential components to its witness to the world. As David Augsburger writes:

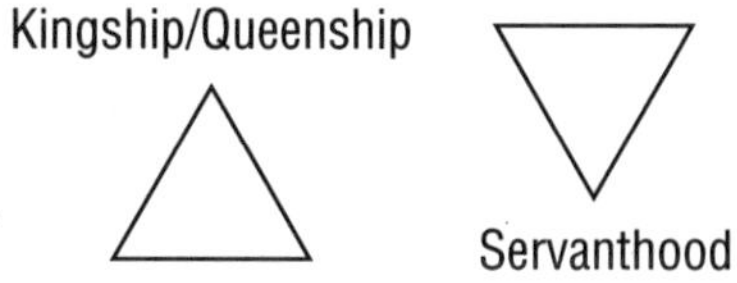

The Upside-Down Kingdom of God

> The church is an alternative community–an alternative to human communities that live by coercion, competition and collective self-interest. It seeks to be a community of disciples who obey the particular ways of God that are revealed in Jesus. It models neighbor love, transformative redemptive justice, inclusion of the stranger, servanthood to each other and beyond, creative love, forgiveness and reconciliation and the humility to recognize and confess its own need for repentance and forgiveness.[2]

This new society is shaped by the virtues and disciplines revealed in the words of Jesus in the Sermon on the Mount (Mt. 5). What the world needs to see is the authenticity, wonder, and beauty of people so captivated with the life of God that they cannot help but practice their faith by living authentic lives. It is a call to be people distinct and identifiable from the world (2 Cor. 6:16–18), demonstrating a frail humanity that witnesses to the life-giving nature of God.

Called out for a purpose, these people are also called to be a community of common participation in which the faithful are bound together not just by belief in dogma but because of their communion with God. The church is a people who, as a community, experience and flesh out Christ's love, grace, and forgiveness.

Acts provides an amazing illustration of what life in the community of the Spirit means. The sudden startling descent of the Spirit in Acts 2 interrupts the disciples caught in the chaotic relational friction brought on by the death and resurrection of Christ. The Spirit forms a common community of purpose and relational connectivity. Believers come together as a fellowship of faith empowered to live together in such a way as to have all things shared in common (Acts 2:42–47).

To be a community of faith is to understand the sacred life that either authenticates the words we speak or causes them to be empty and hollow. This is our biggest challenge. We have been transforming congregations into audiences, proclamation into performance, and worship into entertainment. Quantitative growth, while essential to the life of the church, was too often the measurement of choice without the balancing tension of qualitative growth that evaluated the character and depth of the gospel's incorporation into the lives of the individuals and their lives together. Saying "yes" to Jesus is only one decision in a long journey of discipleship. Living as kingdom people is much more difficult. It means living daily both individually and corporately as if God is in charge, even when reality may appear otherwise.

It is in the church that we see a glimpse of the enormous potential of the upside-down kingdom of God, where the first shall be last, the least shall be greatest, and where those without hope begin to dream dreams again. Here the person far from God finds forgiveness, the outsider finds a place to belong, and those who in the eyes of the world are nothing find possibilities in the affirmation of God.

"Called Together": What Is This Community Like?

Christianity in the New Testament was profoundly rooted in the formation of a new community–the church. The radical nature of the Christian faith in the first century was as much about the church and its formation as it was about the personal experience of the individual. It was first and foremost the creation of a new community, a new way of relating together in our humanity, which resulted in a people who "were one in heart and mind… and shared everything they had" (Acts 4:32–35, NIV).

I was starkly reminded of this truth during a recent gathering of friends at our home. We were introducing some longtime friends to a new one from the Southern United States whom we had met recently. This wonderful Southern gentleman had been involved in a community development program. He and a group of believers have pinpointed ten of the poorest counties in the United States and begun an incarnational presence of capacity building and ministry development.

It was an exciting conversation as he discussed what they were doing and the ways in which it was changing him. At one point, one of our friends asked this Southern gentleman when he had developed a social conscience. Immediately a rebuttal question was posed to the questioner by another friend, "Ah, when was it that you became a Christian?"

Our friend who posed the first question paused for only a moment, turned to the other, and said, "That is exactly right; it is part of faith and discipleship," and the conversation took off from there as we mused over the ways we as North American followers of Christ have watered down the radical and revolutionary nature of the call of the gospel.

When did you get a social conscience? When did you become a Christian? These are great questions. It is intriguing to reflect on how we began to think that working for justice for the poor and the disempowered was a special call. I am aware that some have taken the other side and considered the social concern aspects of the Christian life the primary concern for all they do. Somehow we began to think that one aspect of the gospel was more crucial than the other. Both single-sided approaches appear to miss the mark.

Church historians can answer the question as to how the shifts in emphasis happened: How it is that we began to push one agenda over the other? How is it that we strayed from the whole of God's purpose for the church? They can also tell us that a thread of radical Christianity has always existed down through the centuries in which revolutionary disciples hold in tension a compassionate concern for justice with an evangelistic zeal for people to encounter Christ.

I am more intrigued by the following: the call to faithful engagement in our world has become an "if you get around to it" kind of thing. After involvement in our small group during the week, the varied commitments to the church committees, worship team, and church fellowship–*then,* if we have time, we should be concerned. It is intriguing to think that we have begun to view discipleship in its fullest form as an elective course and not part of the core curriculum.

Some may take offense at these comments. They are likely well-intentioned believers who sponsor a child on a regular basis or do something special at Christmas such as put together a shoebox for a child somewhere around the world. They may even volunteer at an inner-city soup kitchen or ministry of compassion. But think about it. Do these people consider these activities part of the entire package of what it means to be follower of Jesus Christ, or do they perceive them as "add ons" that make them feel as if they are doing the extra after the commitments to the real disciplines are fulfilled? Are these actions really transformational, or are they simply making the status quo more palatable?

David Fitch believes that living out the reign of God's declaration of complete sovereignty is the key challenge for twenty-first–century believers. Followers of Jesus Christ have declared that Jesus is Lord, but words are not enough, as Fitch says; living out our witness of that truth is crucial in contemporary times. He states it this way:

> The question is, how do we make sense of the Christian claim that "Jesus is Lord" in a postmodern world where old ways to truth have broken down? The answer is we display what these words mean in the way we live and worship so that its reality, once displayed, cannot be denied, only rejected or entered into. We will persuade through living displays of truth, not rational one-on-one arguments.[3]

God calls the church, the community of common participation, to embody this truth, acknowledging that where Jesus is Lord people's values and virtues are different. These differences are profoundly felt when the church engages the culture around it. Philip Kenneson and James Street speak to this challenge as well in the realization that, while seeker-sensitive strategies framed a way of looking at the community, they produced market-driven strategies that were not necessarily shaped around the understanding of the church and its mission:

> It [the church] has forgotten why God has called it to be a sign, a foretaste, and a herald of God's new creation. What it needs most, therefore, is a new and powerful vision of what God has called it to be in the world. We think that Rene Padilla has offered just such a powerful vision: The missiology that the church needs today is not one that conceives the people of God as a quotation taken from the surrounding society,

> but one that conceives it as an embodied question-mark that challenges the values of the world.[4]

Stanley Hauerwas and William Willimon, in their book *Resident Aliens,* challenge us to be influencers in the world as the church *by being the church*:

> By being the church, that is, by being something the world is not and can never be, lacking the gift of faith and vision, which is ours in Christ. The confessing church seeks the visible church, a place, clearly visible to the world in which people are faithful to their promises, love their enemies, tell the truth, honor the poor, suffer for righteousness and thereby testify to the amazing community-creating power of God. The confessing church has no interest in withdrawing from the world, but it is not surprised when its witness evokes hostility for the world... This church knows that its most credible form of witness (and the most "effective" thing it can do for the world) is the actual creation of a living, breathing, visible community of faith.[5]

A friend of mine was asked at his ordination examination to explain the meaning of the "priesthood of all believers." The ordination council, Baptist in orientation, was nervous that his Presbyterian roots would prove inadequate in its understanding of what they thought was a uniquely Baptist belief.

Having anticipated this question, my friend chuckled. He commented that he knew what they wanted him to say but that he thought it meant much more than that. It was not just the ability to approach God individually without the assistance of the priest but a call to community where we are priests to one another.

That day, he captured in the fullest sense a part of our sacred identity as the people of God. We are called to be priests to one another in the community of faith–purveyors of God's grace, love, and forgiveness who put action to the character of God. We must often be reminded that one of the ways people experience the grace and forgiveness of God is through you and me.

This is why the idea of a common community of participation is so crucial to our understanding of what it means to be the church. Our life together reflects who God is and how God works through us.

"Called For": How Will This Community Function?

I remember overhearing a conversation between our church's youth minister and several of her peers from other churches. Our

Sunday morning service was highly liturgical, with robes and written liturgy, while the evening service was quite nontraditional. Both services worked well and proved effective in their contemporary content while being framed in particular styles. These young pastors from other churches had little appreciation for the traditional style of worship and as a consequence were taunting her about the clergy robe she wore on Sunday mornings.

I found myself indignantly intervening on her behalf and querying them on their historic church involvement. I asked how many of them had grown up in the church and was not surprised to see them all raise their hands. I have learned that much of what so-called edgy pastors view as radical is too often derived by their reaction to their childhood experiences of church. They think being radical and cutting edge is as easy as throwing out the hymn book, when all they have done is change the music. The community of faith must function at a much deeper level than simply what worship style it chooses to adopt.

Images, as proposed at the beginning of this chapter, can help to reveal a church's implicit theology. They function in such a way as to enable members to describe and convey an impression of something that the community holds central.

Avery Dulles wrote *Models of the Church,* a book that has become the classic source for studies on the ecclesiastical images that people hold dear.[6] He develops thematic categories that appear to help members identify their vision for the church. Each thematic category can stand alone, and each contains both strengths and weaknesses. Each image derives clear implications as to the way people will envision ministry and even their own personal participation and commitment within the church.

- The institutional model perceives the church as a foundational cornerstone in society, emphasizing its continuity with the past. Participation in the church perpetuates this reality by developing structures that sustain the church's continued existence.
- The community model takes an extremely high view of life together as the community of faith. This emphasis on the relational nature of the church focuses on the quality of community fellowship and care.
- The sacramental model captures the idea of the church embodying a sign of God's graceful presence. Here the church sees itself as a sign of God in the world. Its life together serves as a witness for all to see.
- The kerygmatic model sees the church as a proclaiming herald of the good news, in which members are responsible for finding

places to witness to their faith. This is the image of the voice in the wilderness proclaiming the words of good news.

- Not all that different in emphasis, but distinct in method from the kerygmatic model, is the diaconal model. While the former image stresses the use of words, the latter emphasizes the incarnational presence of the people of God called to bear witness to their faith in acts of kindness and servanthood. To the world, the church is an agent of justice and compassion.

Dulles does hold a preference for one image, which he believes pulls all of the attributes of the other images together: the church as a *community of disciples.* He sees the gathered community of believers living as a colony of faith, offering a taste of what it might be like if God reigned in the world. The life of the congregation is not culminated in its gathering together in worship, because that is only one aspect of its call to be the church. Followers are also called to scatter into the world in both proclamation and servant deeds that witness to the gospel call on their lives. Word and deed, gathered and scattered, the church is imaged as a gathering of disciples living a distinct and special purpose.

Dulles' thematic images have been helpful when consulting with congregations. It has been important to coax out the predominant images at work in the minds of the members of the church. It is fascinating to watch as people react to each description. A slight nod of a head or the twitch of a smile telegraphs which image they affirm.

After the image is identified, the next challenge is to investigate the implications that emerge from each image. I often ask the participants to jot down answers to the following questions:

- What sort of congregational environment does this image suggest?
- What is its predominant view of the gospel?
- What is the role of the church members through this image?
- What is the role of the minister/pastor? Of leadership?
- How is ministry perceived?
- How is ministry evaluated for effectiveness?

The problem with personally held images of the church is that they serve as latent assumptive bases from which members make decisions and priorities, anticipate what should take place, and expect how clergy and laity should function in ministry. These influential assumptions too often go unexamined and unarticulated. How we image the church directly affects our approach to ministry, the way we develop strategies and programs, and the way we visualize relationships with one another inside the congregation and outside in the community of neighborhoods. Time-bound images shaped within a particular historical time can make churches prisoners to all their ensuing implications. They can encroach on our ability to respond to proposed changes, particularly if the assumed predominant image is no longer relevant.

Unarticulated and unexamined personal images of the church can prove to be destructive in congregational life. Assuming a theology of the church can prove extremely dangerous because the question is not about what *you* think the church should be. The real question is, What does *God* intend the church to be? What does God want the church to become?

"Called To": Why Does This Community Exist?

Whatever the church is, it is first and foremost God's newness to the world. It is God's alternative community: distinct politically, relationally, morally, and ethically seeking to live differently and relevantly together. Emil Brunner once wrote that the greatest loss for the church was the fact that it had "lost its power of newness."

This idea of the church as God's new creation emerges quickly in the New Testament and this idea has deep and profound implications. From the new commandment given by Jesus to "love one another" (Jn. 15:9–17) to the story in Luke 4 in which Jesus takes up the challenge of fulfilling the prophetic words of Isaiah 61, the announcement of the kingdom and an age to come embodied by values of justice, righteousness, and hope framed this new creation God is forming through Jesus. The Galilean commissions his disciples into the world with the same mandate that he was given by God: to understand that sometimes they will be out of step with the world around them (Jn. 15:18ff). The late Stan Grenz captured this powerful image of God's new thing when he wrote:

> The church is not an end in itself. God does not call us out of the world to become a cozy little clique of a "holy huddle." Rather the church exists to serve a larger intention. The Spirit forms us into a people through whom he can bring about the completion of God's work in the world. This suggests that we must be a future oriented people. Our task is directed toward a grand goal which will come into its fullness only at the end of the age... To understand this, we must introduce the biblical drama of God at work establishing the kingdom or reign. Indeed, the church initially emerged in the context of Jesus' announcement. "The kingdom of God is near" (Mk. 1:15).[7]

The newness of God is framed in our call as the church to be representatives of the new way of living together: a way of life bounded by love and service to one another and the willingness to pour ourselves out into the world; a new ethic that leads us to live together as a community of faith in ways not yet possible outside of this community. This call is what Grenz means when he writes about the establishment of the reign of God.

Our participation in the reign of God can be understood as joining the adventurous passionate rhythm of God's activity. It is a rhythm of three themes that constantly serve as the undertone of borderland existence. The rhythm is the beat of being a unique *community* called to display what life as the forgiven and forgiving people of God is really like, the beat of *witness* to the transformational nature of God, and the beat of *service* in the world in we are placed.

The ministry of the church is always strengthened by a commitment to the transformational power of community. The first beat in the rhythm, commitment to *community,* confirms the truth that witness is never complete without a community of believers who give illustration to what life is like in the shared life of love and faith. A community of faith living at the grassroots level day to day bearing with others, serving in love and forgiving in the context of the grace of the gospel as described by Paul in Colossians, is a powerful example of what God is doing through the gift of the kingdom come to earth (Col. 2:12 and following).

This sacred trust of God's message of hope takes place in the context of real people–cranky, headstrong, and conflicted, but seeking what is best and good. The church's acceptance of the marginal binds us strangely to the gospel call for all people to have place and belonging. Multiple cultures living together with love, purpose, and hope serve as a beacon of hope for what it might be like to live as a global community committed to God.

I suspect that most of us grew up with highly individualistic views of Christianity. It was Jesus and me. Walter Brueggemann's *Cadences of Home* is provocative, prophetic, and insightful in speaking against this type of gospel living. He examines models of the church in scripture and concludes that the model dominating modern experience is that which arose during the Israelite monarchy, a relatively short period in Israel's history. The conditions that produced this individualistic model and made it workable at the time were swept away in a cultural geopolitical upheaval.

> Ezra is the great "new Church start" leader. A new Church means reformulating the faith in radical ways in the midst of

> a community that has to begin again. For Ezra, as for Moses, new Church starts do not aim at strategies for success, but at strategies for survival of an alternative community. What must survive is not simply the physical community; what must survive is an alternative community with an alternative memory and an alternative social perspective rooted in a peculiar text that is identified by a peculiar genealogy and signed by peculiar sacraments, by peculiar people not excessively beholden to the empire and not lusting after domestication into the empire.[8]

The concept of a visible community in this world fueled the identity of the people of Israel. They believed they were called to be a community that belongs to God and a witness to God's presence in history and to God's reign over all things. The vision of God's peace, spread over all God's creation, opened the door to a glorious vision of history.

The second beat of the rhythm of God's reign is *witness* to the transformational nature of the gospel in both word and deed. Church traditions perceive this idea of witnessing differently. For some, the context is evangelism and the Word proclaimed. For others, it is the Word lived out in acts of compassion and justice. For decades, this theme has been the motivating force for the missionary movement and what many mean by "doing mission."

Words, however, are not enough. Witness is more than words. Words are authenticated by incarnational living of the gospel in the everyday lives of followers of Christ. At this time in church history, it is difficult to find places where the holistic ministry of Word and deed is not affirmed. The problem is that, for many, one aspect of witnessing is more important than the other, producing a pale image of the gospel lived out. Situation and context frames the witness response but gospel-valued living, compassionate ministry, and proclamation dialogue form an integral whole.

The last beat of the rhythm of God's reign is that of sacrificial compassionate *service*. This is the church at work, representing the reign of God among its neighbors near and far. The life and teachings of Jesus reveal a call of the people who follow him to see themselves as representatives of God's reign living as a community both as messenger (witness) and servant. Guder points out that the presence and the deeds of Jesus were both signposts and signatures pointing to God, which are now lived out through the life and mission of the church.[9]

To realize mission, all three themes must be present. However, before the church is called to do or say something, it is called and sent to be the unique community of those who live under the reign of God. Being transformed into a living, breathing, redeemed body of Christ under the reign of Christ is essential to the missional call. The church displays the first fruits of the forgiven and forgiving people of God who are brought together across the rubble of dividing walls that have crumbled under the weight of the cross.

Being the visible and recognizable covenant community that shows the tangible character of God's reign in human and social form is usually more of a challenge than appropriately contextualizing the gospel message in our culture. In our highly individualized culture, we do not often choose to live together in inconvenience and discomfort. For the church, however, this inconvenient life together is crucial.

Living, no matter how haltingly, as an alternative, countercultural, biblical community of reconciliation is the call of God's reign. Recovering our missional soul will probably mean stopping as many things that we usually think of as church as it means starting new ones. The ongoing process of consolidating our lives so we can actually live in community as God's people under his reign will be the difficult work.

We must discover and imagine what it means to be church in the particular neighborhood and context to which we have been called. This requires being organic instead of institutional, and emphasizing people rather than places, community rather than meetings, movements on a mission rather than building of a membership. The church is better understood as a people, a community, a way of life, a way of connectedness with other Christ followers in the world.

The "go" motivation decentralizes the local congregation, fanning out into local neighborhoods and communities. Through service and witness the body of Christ becomes a reality. Leading the people of God to possibilities of incarnational *community, witness,* and sacrificial compassionate *service* provides a full witness in representing the reign of God.

The Church as a Borderland Community

Living the rhythms of the reign of God assumes that the people of God are a missionary people. This incredible truth has been unpacked more thoroughly in the previous chapter, but it needs to be understood that this "*missio deo*" is inherent in what God intended as the church. It flows from and is consistent with the missionary nature of God. It calls God's people to the same orientation, moving the church from simply seeing itself as a gathering of people and a sender of select missionaries to the affirmation of the church itself as being sent.

Darrell Guder believes that it has taken decades for Christians caught up in the old "come to" strategies of the past to understand that mission is not just a program. If we imagine the church as God's sent people, we are either defined by mission or choose something else as our definition. We are either framed by our "go to" sentness and see the borderlands as the place of our involvement on a daily basis, or we live insular religiously institutional lives. Guder writes, "our challenge today is to move from church with mission to missional church."[10] Indeed, he goes on to say "the main business of many mission committees (where mission became only one of the many programs of the church), is to determine how to spend the mission budget rather than view the entire congregational budget as an exercise in mission."[11]

If the church, wherever it is geographically, is to "be mission" and not just "do mission," some key characteristics must be present in what it does. The best way to understand the significance of God's mission is to study its culmination in the coming of Jesus. Christ came to announce and demonstrate the present and coming kingdom of God. Under God's reign in Christ, the whole world has been redeemed to God. "The church's mission," Robert Webber therefore states, "is to be the presence of the kingdom."[12] The implications of these theological themes woven together into a passionate missionary purpose as a sent people of God to the world are enormous.

Lesslie Newbigin makes a distinction between the *missionary dimension* of the church and the church's *missionary intention.*[13] The missionary *dimension* of a local church's life manifests itself, among other ways, when

- It is truly a worshiping community
- It is able to welcome outsiders and make them feel at home
- The pastor does not have the monopoly on the ministry of the church
- Members are not merely objects of pastoral care
- Members are equipped for ministry in the community
- It is structurally pliable and innovative
- It does not defend the privileges of a select few

The church becomes *intentional* as a missionary people when:

- It is directly involved in the community/society
- It moves beyond the walls of the church to "points of concentration"

- It evangelizes
- It works for justice
- It is involved in the alleviation of suffering
- It works for peace

These missionary dimensions and its intentional actions developed by Newbigin are helpful in understanding what is our call as the church. They encourage practical and conceptual aspects to the conversation and strategy building by imagining the broad themes of the task and then measuring the nature of the missional existence of the congregation through the lens of activity and orientation.

God's Intent: A Borderland People

The wave of the future in Christ's church will be built on people who both understand the sacred and high privilege of being a called out community peculiarly living a life of virtue together and, at the same time, are willing to pour themselves out to the world. They are a people so caught up in their missional task of participating in God's work in the borderlands that they want nothing else to do but live it out. These are a people who no longer see some places as secular and others as sacred because they realize that all territories are sacred places where God is at work.

These passionate people are mobilized and energized by the implications of the gospel on their lives in such a way as to seek to be a people of kingdom ethics empowered by the Spirit to live differently both as a community and as people in the world. Thoughtfully, they desire to apply all the values and virtues of Christ's reign in the context in which God has placed them. Paul captures this mind-set of a borderland people when, in 2 Corinthians 10:3–5, he writes:

> For though we live in the world, we do not wage war as the world does. The weapons we fight with are not the weapons of the world. On the contrary, they have divine power to tear down strongholds. We demolish arguments and every pretension that sets itself up against the knowledge of God and we take captive every thought to make it obedient to Christ. (NIV)

They are a people so moved by the Spirit of God to live differently that they create an atmosphere in which people ask, "Who is this God you serve?" Anticipating God is at work and so passionately desiring to be part of it, these people look for God in all the things that they do. Marva Dawn says they "don't work to change the world, they work to anticipate the Kingdom." Mary Jo Leddy says it another way, "The future will belong to those who have nothing to lose."[14]

A REST STOP ALONG THE WAY

- Engage in your own study of the Ephesian church. Compare what you learn with your own current church context.
- What has been your dominant image of the church–as institution, as community, as sacrament, or as herald? Unpack the implications of each image by discussing answers to the questions listed earlier in the chapter.
- Describe in your own words God's intent for the church. Explain why the metaphor of the borderland does or does not capture God's intent.

4

Landscapes and Tool Kits

The Challenge of Borderland Leading

BORDERLAND COMPASS POINT

Leaders of today's borderland churches are living on a new pastoral landscape and require a new tool kit of strategies comprised of a new understanding of their role, an honest evaluation of themselves, and the ability to create a variety of secure places of relationships. They image their leadership in the frames of apprentice-pastor-theologian-missionary. Borderland leaders must embody the apostle Paul's understanding of leadership as expressed in the first letter to the Thessalonians–sharing not only the gospel of God but their lives as well (1 Thess. 2:17–20).

I was late, and traffic was not being helpful. I burst into the waiting room of the hospital with a bit too much energy. I had promised this young teenager in our church that I would pray with her before her operation. Breathlessly, I said to the nurse, "I am Gary Nelson, pastor of FBC. I am here to see Laurie before she goes in for her operation."

"How do I know you are a pastor?" the nurse said, holding her hand up to hold me back. "You haven't got a pastoral care security badge on."

It was true. Having always had an aversion to name badges, I never pursued actually getting the hospital visitation badge required for all clergy for permission to be on the hospital floors after hours. "Actually I haven't got a badge yet," I said, hoping that she would not ask why. This did not deter her. She asked the next logical question. "Do you have a business card?"

Not being one to use business cards either, I did not have one on me. Sheepishly I replied, "No, I have been meaning to get some reprinted." She looked me over more than once, trying to decide what she should do with me. Finally, she spoke, "Then I can't let you in because I don't know who you are." I was panicking because I had promised. Desperately I grasped at the last arrow in my quiver of excuses and blurted out, "Look, being a pastor in Edmonton is probably one of the most irrelevant occupations in this whole city. Why would I tell you I was the pastor of FBC if I wasn't?"

For a moment, an amused smile came over her face. For me, it was an uncomfortable silence. Then, with a wry chuckle, she replied, "You know, that is a good point. You are probably right both about your irrelevance and about being a pastor. You might as well go in. She could probably use some prayer."

This odd encounter still lives with me, for it captures the reality of the clergy in contemporary North America. Pastoral ministry and church life have been turned upside down and the drastic shifts in the *pastoral landscape* create a fragile vulnerability far different from the pressures of previous decades. Burnout and stress are impacting the profession because of the ambiguity and cross-purposed assumptions experienced.

Combined with new ministry expectations sparked by consumer-driven congregational life, the shifts and pressures strip away the feelings of security that simple faithfulness might evoke. As a result, these times require a vastly different *personal tool kit* for effectiveness. In many cases, seminaries are slow to respond to the changes. Many are only now catching on to the deep abiding shifts required in traditional ministerial education. The critical need is to help clergy create safe and secure places in which they can find rest and from which they can lead as leaders who are socially aware and emotionally intelligent. Unfortunately, the fragile vulnerability of ministering in today's world continues to sweep over many, and the results are dysfunctional congregational systems at work in contemporary church life that both victimize and terrorize many pastors.

"What Is Unique' versus "What Is Normal"

Before we consider more specifically both the *pastoral landscape* and *personal tool kit,* I wish to make an observation regarding clergy life today. I have found fresh insights to the pastoral challenge through the lens of my new role as head of a global mission organization. Reflecting on my past experience as a clergy leader, I have observed missionaries and global Christian workers as they work out the challenges of their ministry and the changing landscapes around them. Mission organizations are exploring care on the mission field in the attempt to learn from past mistakes. The area has become known as "member care," and readings in this area have proven enlightening while, at the same time, frustrating. The vast majority of the literature is written by experts in the profession who themselves were often raised and nurtured in the missionary culture.

Truthfully, I have had only a surface involvement in this culture until now. So, it is not surprising that I look at the content differently than others might. A lack of objectivity and personal insight causes them to miss deeper issues that may be at work in many missionaries' lives. It is strikingly clear that many writers, captured in their own experiences of missionary life, are unable to distinguish between what is *unique* and what is *normal* in the challenges faced by crosscultural workers in the twenty-first century.

For example, the discussion around the area of transitions back from the field to missionaries' original home country, called reentry, contains characteristics that are both *unique* and *normal* in their experience. The *normal* appears to be ignored. Failing to acknowledge the *normal* transitions that anybody would face, whether they are moving from Chicago to Los Angeles or from Nairobi to Toronto, can be extremely dangerous. By failing to make that distinction, the tendency will be to believe that everything experienced in transition is totally *unique.* One believes the experience is like no one else's, and this absolute conviction creates a fragile, isolating, and illusionary pressure. The transition is intensified and the sense of victimization is heightened by a solitude of one's own creation. These same myths are alive in the pastoral ministry.

We may have created our own isolation as clergy and allowed both our training and evaluation of effectiveness through denominational structures to perpetuate it. We may be contributing to our own stress and burnout by buying into the illusionary idea that we are somehow "different." Conviction that the pastoral experience is *unique* makes us believe that our lives are busier, more complex, and more stressful than any others.

The need for deep self-awareness and honesty is inescapable. Without it, we are easily deceived. Eugene Peterson writes, "Deception is nowhere more common than in religion. And the people most easily and damningly deceived are the leaders."[1] If clergy are unaware of the themes that motivate their own lives and ministry, the self-deception and lack of self-awareness plays itself out in the life of the congregation.

The Pastoral Landscape

Many of the trends of leadership change are simply the reality of the contemporary world and its expectations. They impinge on leaders wherever they are. Other issues are unique to the role of pastoral leaders and must be acknowledged as such. Let's first consider issues on today's pastoral landscape.

Irrelevance...as a Unique Place from Which to Live

There was a time when clergy did not need a hospital security badge for identification. They played a significant role in society and were recognized. They were perceived to be relevant and an important part of daily life. The saintly former pastor I introduced in the first chapter had place and significance in the city in the 1950s. He was invited to sit on the board of the professional football team, and business and social leaders conferred with him about municipal concerns. On Monday his sermons were often quoted in the newspaper. Legislative officials often consulted him on major policy decisions about to be made in government. Since the majority of people attended church, the clergy's role was understood and admired.

In most places, this role has disappeared. Where it has not disappeared completely, a gradual and almost imperceptible erosion is taking place. Jeff Woods describes the shift:

> There was a time when a local church pastor was among the most respected and educated people within a community. The pastor seemed to know all of the community movers and shakers. Society held a high regard for the pastoral office. The pastor received a lot of privileges in town, not just from parishioners. Everyone wanted to get on the good side of the local pastor. That is hard to give up. For many, there will be no choice. It will be taken away.[2]

This marginalization began years ago. Its slow march of decline has now combined with recent public clergy moral failures and unethical financial practices to heighten the intensity and speed of erosion. Canadian clergy today are rated as one of the least-trusted occupations. They are perceived to be not far from politicians and lawyers. While fewer people are inclined toward church, the key figure caught in this growing institutional irrelevance is the clergy person. The result is personal and professional dislocation.

Clergy leaders, living with a growing sense of irrelevance, feel an increasing isolation. As those feelings grow, well-meaning clergy find the emotional pressures and role expectations crushing. The result is clergy stress and burnout of epidemic proportions. Irrelevance combined with unrealistic congregational expectations create the "perfect storm" for isolation and lack of ministerial emotional health.

When a clergy leader feels irrelevant outside the walls of the church, such a leader will have more at stake in what happens inside. One's identity, feelings of worth, and significance are placed on a narrow one-dimensional platform. The result is a stark vulnerability not previously experienced in pastoral ministry, causing clergy leaders to put pressure on congregations to meet their needs for significance, needs that are emotionally and relationally unrealistic.

Leaders have more to lose in the everyday rhythms of ministry. Change management, which is difficult in most normal situations, becomes even more difficult in an atmosphere of personal need. Congregational transformation comes with no guarantees and the residual loss of place in the community of faith may be too high a risk. Consequently, conflict is avoided, even subconsciously, because the impact on the congregational network of relationships may be too costly.

Clergy leaders who ground their spiritual, emotional, physical, and psychological needs in one place have a greater potential for feeling victimized by the transitory and constantly shifting nature of ministry. Fearing loss of this one world of significance leads to greater feelings of vulnerability.

***Ambiguity*...of Expectations and Tensions in Roles**

This marginalizing irrelevance is combined with another unique issue–the constant ambiguity of the pastoral ministry. New expectations and demands have emerged over the last decades of congregational life and each has brought a different dimension to the role of minister. John Maxwell challenges us to develop twenty-one characteristics of a "real leader," whereas Brian McLaren challenges us to dialogue with our culture in similar ways as anthropologists. Bill Hybels asks us to be cultural sociologists, seeker-sensitive in our mind-sets. Rob Bell calls us to become postmodern poets while Dallas Willard encourages apprenticeship with Jesus. Marva Dawn and Eugene Peterson want us to stimulate a deeper contemplative spirituality that leads to spiritual companionship with the people of our church.

Congregations reply with their own assortment of sometimes archaic expectations. Often dissonant and incongruent from each other, they appear to have little to do with what the gurus of our discipline are telling us. Be a chaplain or a friend. Be a great preacher and a sensitive liturgist. Above all, grow this church, because if it does not meet my needs, I may choose to go somewhere else.

I remember one of the professors who shaped my thinking of the church speaking to this issue. David Watson was, at that time, the leader of the Anglican Charismatic Renewal. He placed a transparency on an overhead with a picture that displayed a bottle with a stopper in its opening. Written in bold capitalized letters on the stopper was the word *PASTOR*. The implications were clear. The pastor is often the stopper in the bottle, restricting the work of the Spirit and the possibilities of renewal in the church of Jesus Christ.

This was never a comforting thought to me. In fact, I disagreed with David that day in our dialogue. In my experience, it was often church members who resisted congregational transformation and renewal. They had a formal and informal position of power that was unacknowledged in the diagram. We, the pastors, were the converted. We longed for the winds of the Spirit to blow, but so often found ourselves trapped in the congregational attempt to block these fresh breezes.

However, Watson's claim has some truth to it. Pastors are inexplicably joined at the hip with the church and its success or failure. They are the key catalysts for congregational health. Irwin Barker and Don Posterski write: "Whether congregations are large or small, clergy leadership makes the most important difference in why some churches are spirited while others are not… I'm not suggesting that all lethargic congregations find their reset in clergy leadership but clergy leadership makes all the difference."[3]

Whether we like it or not, it rests on clergy. That undeniable reality stimulates irreconcilable pressures placed on ministry today.

How clergy deal with the challenge of irrelevance and ambiguity of expectations is crucial. The greatest need is to develop a grounded personhood and inner compass of measurement. These are critical to the ability to navigate and negotiate the constant barrage of expectations. They will have a direct result on the life of the congregation, but, more importantly, they will create space from which clergy can lead confidently and securely.

Realistically, most of the strain and crisis in leadership today are found in our inability to navigate and negotiate these ambiguous and complex worlds of expectations, professional marginalization, and faulty conceptual foundations. This is partly why clergy health and leadership burnout issues are epidemic today.

Other reasons also exist as to why this is the case. The most obvious is the inability of leaders to become the solutions for their own struggles in the church. Loren Mead writes, "Clergy are a critical part of the problem. Many of them are uncomfortably aware of that fact."[4] Like the quarterback of the football team, they are perceived to be either the great implementer of the church's success or the reason for the church's decline.

Certainly some of the solutions can be discovered through thoughtful reflection on what is at work in these unhealthy situations. However, it is my conviction that we as clergy leaders must develop more realistic and healthy patterns of living.

Accessing...Too Much Information

Being informed is highly overrated. Clergy leaders study the trends and read every book on the church that is offered, including this one. They attend the seminars offered to help clergy and church leaders envision and manage ministries more effectively. The result in some cases is information overload.

I meet pastors regularly who can articulate a vision for what they hope and believe for the church. They have been given words to express their hopes, analyze their culture, and present a future. Models have provided frames for their visioning. They know, sadly, what *should* happen, but somehow are unable to get there. The result is pastors focused on techniques for manipulating and motivating others rather than dealing with the emotional and communal processes. Key to healthy borderland ministry is the clergy leader rooted and resting in an inner emotional and social community awareness that allows for leadership to take place.

Diverse...Images of the Church

The cultural shifts of the twenty-first century have affected the way we image the church. Our beliefs and images of what the church should be have powerful implications. As discussed in chapter 3, when congregational members and clergy image church in different ways, dissonant expectations are the result. If this were simply a theological exercise, then it would make the shaping of borderland churches into missional expressions easier. But it is more than this.

The church is a human institution and system. Shaped by their experience, people become part of churches for a variety of reasons. They bring complex expectations and assumptions into their life together. Pastors, caught in these unexamined views of congregational life and bound with the congregation's lack of an effective ecclesiology, must have the relational skill set, the spiritual rootedness, and emotional grounding to navigate the white waters of conflict.

In some congregations, the most dependent members of the church are allowed to set the agendas. Adaptation is constantly toward weakness rather than strength, and the recalcitrant and passively aggressive leverage power. When anxious and dysfunctional members of the church frame the focus of life together, the result is that energetic, visionary, imaginative, and creatively motivated members are ignored.

Seminaries and Bible colleges emphasize the academic and intellectual content required to access the theological knowledge framed in the Christendom model of pastoral formation. Many seminaries fail to nurture the spiritual, social, and relational intelligence required to lead effective congregational life. It could be argued that neither practical theology nor ministry supervision experiences are shaped in such a way as to change these realities. They have led us into journeys of psychological self-discovery and well-being that are too individual in nature, failing to acknowledge the "we of me" that makes us people of community systems and the call of ministry leadership to be communitarian.

Pastoral leaders who lack the ability to access the joy and life of communitarian living end up isolated. Without a nurtured relational and social intelligence, they observe conflict and resistance as anomalies rather than realities of life in community. Their widespread misunderstanding about the relational nature of church life causes them to assume that toxic forces can be regulated through reasonableness, love, insight, role-modeling, inculcation of values, and striving for consensus, when they should be taking the kinds of stands that set limits to the invasiveness of those who lack self-regulation.

This reality alone is daunting, but it can be made worse when pastoral leaders bring faulty personal expectations to the task. How we image our role as clergy in normal organizational and church life has a direct result on our inner health. Healthy imaging eventually sees that "resistance," as it is usually perceived, is part and parcel of the systemic process of leadership.[5]

Relationships...Are Critical

The importance of genuine relationships is now understood as a crucial aspect for all leaders. It has arisen from a growing distrust of public figures. Congregational members expect interpersonal maturity from a minister and they look for a quality of relationship that provides a window into the real life of their clergy leaders. A genuine relationship with the clergy person, rather than the role he or she plays, allows them to trust. Relational trust is linked with influence. Mike Regele writes, "Authority in the future will be granted to people, not to positions. It will not be enough, and indeed will most likely be counterproductive, to claim authority based upon position."[6]

Leadership is first and foremost an act of authentic connection within a community of relationships. Individualistic leadership styles that once dominated our culture are becoming passé. This focused individual is being replaced by the self-questioning servant style leaders who see themselves as part of a network of relationships. They are connected to others on whom they rely for strength, clarity, and purpose.

This communitarian view of leadership has been the preferred theological model, but for decades the pastor as CEO has dominated the frames of church-based pastoral ministry. Leadership was perceived to be an individual and somewhat lonely pursuit. This leadership style had mild success for some but was frustrating to others. Its strength was its ability to build audiences, but its weakness was the struggle for community building. Leonard Hjalmarson goes so far as to say it is damaging to organic and communal life. He writes that it tends to "build congregations rather than communities, buildings rather than temples of living stones, and audiences rather than families of faith."[7] A different set of skills is required for building communities that are genuinely transparent and it will only be those places that can be effective frameworks for borderland living. Clay Shirsky writes about it:

> [Building a community] will require different skills and attitudes than those necessary to build an audience. Many of the expectations you make about the size, composition, and behavior of audiences when you are in a broadcast mode are actually damaging to community growth. To create an environment conducive to real community, you will have to operate more like a gardener than an architect.[8]

One would think that clergy would love to jettison the idea of the pastor as CEO leader, but this is not the case. The pastor as CEO is very seductive in what it promises and allows clergy a distance in relationship that some believe will shield them as leaders from the vulnerability inherent in leadership today. However, there will not be an option for most of us. Leadership in this new millennium will be essentially framed in relationships, which acknowledge the web of dependency so crucial for community development.

Not surprisingly, the apostle Paul appeared to understand this actuality. His writings, while ancient, are contemporary in their awareness of the relational dimension of ministry. He writes to the church of Thessalonica about this subject. The first two chapters are written as a defense against those who question his authority and his ministry in general. His defense is a relational one, discussing his ministry style and motivation. He puts it this way, "We loved you so much that we were delighted to share with you not only the gospel of God but our lives as well, because you had become so dear to us" (1 Thess. 2:8, NIV).

Paul puts up a marvelous defense by saying, "You know who I am and how I lived among you." It is, however, an approach that could dismally fail if the words are dissonant to the truth of the Thessalonians' experience of Paul. All they would need to say is, "We were never dear to you," and his apology would disintegrate. In this is found both the power of the relational model of leadership and its' unfortunate Achilles' heel.

Release...Christendom's View of the Church

Somewhere along this journey we lost what it means to be the church. It is not the purpose of this book to analyze why this took place.[9] Institutionalized and insular views of church life made us unable to engage culture in significant ways when those cultures and societies began to change. Borderland living was optional and churches found definition in their internal congregational activities.

We failed to challenge these institutionalized Christendom foundations about church. Instead, we attempted to work with cosmetic alterations of how we packaged church, tailoring ourselves with more contemporary clothes in the desperate hope that the borderland people will find us more attractive.

Tragically, we lost our compass and settled too often for pale imitations of what church really could be. The challenge was to examine our core beliefs about church, but we did not show up for the discussion. It really is a simple question, one that has been asked by every generation. How you answer the question implicates everything you do.

The implications that emerge from the answers to these questions are enormous. Leaders of the church caught in the models of success placed before them are trapped. If they do not examine these models in the light of theological and biblical views of the church, they will become victims of every fad. Models are only helpful if rooted in a deep abiding theology of the church–understanding why it exists and what mission God, in his passionate purposefulness, set it to do.

Pastors and church leaders lacking a grounded theology of the church live in a panicky obsession with data and technique. Data and technique junkies find themselves caught in an obsession with "managerial missiology."[10] This approach enables leaders to focus on the quantitative and cosmetic frameworks of strategy and programs while avoiding the theological, relational, and content-oriented processes that are the places where visions and dreams are realized.

The Personal Tool Kit

While studying at Fuller seminary, I attended a course on the shaping of the interior emotional, psychological, and spiritual life of the minister. Dr. Archibald Hart was the insightful teacher who wove his knowledge as a psychologist and experience as an immigrant from South Africa into his work with clergy over many years. He described the pastoral life in the context of a diamond. He observed that clergy's lives are often "one-dimensionally faceted" and, consequently, an inordinate amount of pressure is placed on that solitary facet. Healthy leaders, we were told, "multi-facet" their lives in the healthful conviction that when one area of their lives is not going well, the other facets provide balance.

Edgar Friedman provides deep insight concerning leadership formation and self-understanding. In a book entitled *A Failure of Nerve*, he states that leadership "has less to do with the specificity of given problems, the nature of a particular technique, or the make-up of a given group. It has more to do with the way everyone is framing the issues."[11] He goes on to say that effective and healthy leaders are well-differentiated people. His definition of differentiated leadership is quite clear:

> I mean someone who has clarity about his or her own life goals and therefore, someone who is less likely to become lost in the anxious emotional processes swirling about. I mean someone who can be separate while still remaining connected

> and therefore can maintain a modifying, non-anxious, and sometimes challenging presence. I mean someone who can manage his or her own reactivity to the automatic reactivity of others and therefore be able to take stands at the risk of displeasing. It is not as though some leaders can do this and some cannot. No one does this easily and most leaders can improve their capacity.[12]

Healthy and effective leadership requires more than technique. It is a lifelong process of spiritual and emotional discipline that enables leaders to keep balance. Friedman believes that these spiritual and emotional disciplines are difficult to develop because they require the capacity to become oneself. This is probably never fully achieved because it refers to a direction in life rather than a state of being.[13] Friedmann believes that this place of differentiation enables the leader:

- To find the capacity to take a stand in an intense emotional system
- To contain one's reactivity to the reactivity of others, which includes the ability to avoid being polarized
- To maintain a nonanxious presence in the face of anxious others
- To know where self ends and the other begins
- To be able to cease automatically being one of the system's emotional dominoes
- To be clear about one's own personal values and goals
- To be responsible for one's own emotional being and destiny rather than blaming others or the context

These are foundational necessities for Christian leadership. Leadership is most effective when it emerges from rooted security and safety. Gordon Macdonald calls these characteristics "below the waterline issues" of spiritual formation and Christian identity in Jesus Christ.[14]

We often pay lip service to the need to develop these characteristics. To live healthfully in intense ambiguity and marginalization, one must be strongly rooted. For borderland leaders, this means dwelling deeply in Christ. Eugene Peterson and Marva Dawn describe the challenge this way:

> As we become good at leadership, we become used to people following us. They look to us for direction, expect initiative from us, and not infrequently turn over responsibility for their lives to us, expecting us to take up the slack that results from their indolence and passivity. Leaders usually work

> harder than followers. Leaders characteristically accept more responsibility than followers. Sometimes the followers admire us, others times they criticize us, but in either case we are made aware that we are being treated as a class apart; we are leaders... It is a subtle thing and usually takes years to accomplish, but without "protection"–without that piton hammered into the rock face–the role of leaders almost inevitably replaces the role of follower. Instead of continuing as followers of the Lord Jesus Christ, we become bosses on behalf of the Lord Jesus Christ.[15]

Lead...with Your Story

A seminary professor was discussing his perspectives on preaching during a seminary class. He queried his students about the preaching task with two questions. "What is preaching?" he asked, and, "What is it all about?" Our answers were typically full of theological and academic words. Caught in the lofty places of higher learning, we wanted to make it more intellectual and inaccessible. He listened patiently for a while but finally interrupted our wordy intellectualizations with a simple and profound statement, "Preaching is God's story in your story." Then he asked, "Ah! But what if there is no story?"

Healthy and effective borderland leaders find their rootedness in "God's story" as it relates to their unfolding story of church and community engagement. This narrative shapes the way they lead and creates the canvas on which outcomes of their leadership are painted. As they model an integration of personal spiritual encounter and relevant community living, the congregation develops its ability to live out that same integration.

I live in a country that negatively images aggressive and proactive leadership. We like our leaders to be somewhat reluctant and unassuming. Some covet the "can do" atmosphere so prevalent in the United States. Whatever your preferred contextual leadership image, the key part of the journey is where deep spiritual disciplines are developed and from which the risk of leadership can take place. These risks must take place if a church community with varied expectations, role confusions, and preferred directions is to move ahead.

In *Future Faith Churches,*[16] Don Posterski and I called this idea "leading from soul." If leaders are called to transform congregations into spiritually dynamic borderland movements, it will be necessary for them to discern and nurture their own souls. Professional expertise is not enough.

Concerning this living and leading from their soul, Gordon Macdonald, reflecting on the "below the waterline" issues of life, writes, "The soul is the deeper part of all of us that others cannot see. It is a quiet place where people are most apt to connect with God. In that deeper, quiet piece of spiritual geography there was, in biblical times and is today, dialogue with heaven events of repentance, praise... and the formation of intentions to life and knowledge that enable people to become what I like to call kingdom builders."[17]

We see hints of the amazing capacities that God meant all of us to have as we secure ourselves in that resting place. It is the product of the indwelling Spirit of God that comes to replace the deadened parts of our own lives.

Borderland leaders enter into that story. Word, Spirit, and community nurture their souls, bringing a unique understanding of spirituality to the leadership task. Secular management consultants Lee Bolman and Terence Deal describe it this way: "The signs point toward spirit and soul as the essence of leadership."[18] If ignored, the result is a hollow leader, someone who spends most of life and ministry responding to events and circumstances rather than living through them.

Living from the soul of leadership provides the intangible characteristics and qualities that set leadership apart. Their soul capacity creates a grounded place from which they can find courage to risk and lead. Without it, life is shallow and the nerve to lead almost impossible to conjure up.

The result is a leadership style more rooted in character development than learned technical skills. Inner development of character focused on themes such as integrity, honesty, humility, courage, commitment, sincerity, passion, confidence, wisdom, determination, compassion, and sensitivity are crucial.

Lead...from Transparency

Effective leaders ultimately distinguish themselves by their ability to inspire followers to commit passionately to the cause. Long writes, "We need to make sure that we create an environment in our churches and our Christian fellowships that allows people to become vulnerable enough to share their pain and struggles."[19] By taking up a "what you see is what you get" code of conduct, leaders show respect to the people they are leading and model the possibilities of transparency and honest sharing in the community of faith. This creates credibility and cultivates fertile ground for effective collaboration.

True leadership is built on the type of social contract that says, "Follow me, and I promise that I will help you become something more." If congregations are led to wonder about the hidden agendas of their leaders, distrust has a negative impact on the life of the community of faith. Paul is absolutely emphatic about his motives for leadership. He describes his leadership among the Thessalonians as not having been exercised behind masks of deception. While it is crucial to know how far to go as you transparently open yourself up as a leader, congregations that see nothing of the leader follow with great reluctance.

The reason is simple–peoples' expectations for leadership are rooted in the interpersonal operation of leader-follower relationships. When personal connections are not made through trust, reliability, care, and appreciation, the community has little opportunity to move to a higher level of effectiveness and deeper lives of care.

Congregations desiring credible borderland engagement must work to build genuine community, using strategies that can only emerge through transparent and honest relationships. Genuine community challenges the individualistic tendencies of North American culture. God created us for community, not for disingenuous relationships of insecure needs and aspirations.

***Lead...*from Humility**

Genuinely communal and transparent living is nurtured most effectively through leaders who approach their task with a humble sensibility. Paul speaks to this character attitude as he describes his ministry. It did not emerge from the hollowness of ego needs or the shallowness of playing to the crowd for praise and flattery (1 Thess. 2:5). Everyone needs encouragement and is encouraged by affirmation. However, people who need too much affirmation build the most destructive relationships. This insatiable need for emotional "strokes" is a signal of a leader's insecurity that, if not checked, results in an emotional entrapment. Emotionally dependent leaders will not risk themselves enough to be prophetic in the community of faith. When they choose the prophetic role, too often they are playing to the crowd.

Approaching ministry with humble sensibilities allows the leader to find vision, strength, and creativity within the community of faith. Humble sensibility allows the leader to see people not as the consumers but as those who also are seeking a vision for the church, who also bring gifts to the ministry task. Community building is part of the kingdom-shaping task of borderland living.

Lead...with Sensitivity

Effective leaders bring a character that is sensitive to the task. Paul aptly describes this sensitivity when he tells the Thessalonians that he and his colleagues in ministry were gentle among the people of Thessalonica, in the way a mother nurses her infant (1 Thess. 2:7). It's a wonderful image capturing both the idea of intimacy and the corresponding gentleness of strength. Gentleness in the scriptures is always linked to this concept of controlled strength. Paul's comparison of gentleness to the image of a nursing mother illustrates this dual nature, the hungry infant suckling with eager force while the mother gently coos to her child with calm assurance.

The numerous scriptural references to words such as *patience, long-suffering,* and *steadfastness* portray the quality of relationships possible as a gospel people. Christian community is always lived out in the context of ordinary people carrying varied agendas. Leadership sensitively nurtures this diversity by knowing when to push and when to lay back on issues. They are able to discern the battles that must be fought and those that can be ignored. Sensitive ministry envisions long-term possibilities and therefore creates an environment for growth and deepening.

Jim Collins, in his helpful book *Good to Great,* describes these leaders. He initially uses the term "servant leaders," but, in his discomfort with the word *servant,* he labeled them with the title of Level 5 leaders. These leaders shun celebrity and channel their ambition toward building a great company and, while they have unwavering resolve, they are modest.[20]

The leadership characteristics of humble sensibility and sensitivity enable leaders to gain clarity as they observe their congregations. As shifts and turns take place in one part of community life, they are able to respond quickly because they are secure enough not to be effected by them. They are also not easily frozen by emotional isolation used by some congregational members for manipulation and resistance. Their informed insight about people empowers their ability to navigate and negotiate the ebbs and flows that are natural in the life of a community. It is obvious to them that vision and possibilities emerge from the community and not just the leaders. Borderland leaders are community builders that draw vision, giftedness, and relationships out of the community while warring against the tendency toward going it on their own.

In this cultivated atmosphere, the missional imagination of members emerges in greater clarity. It is a vision that does not come from pre-planned strategies void of dialogue or process, but from the community's shared experience of God moving in its midst. It is revealed not by manipulation but through prayerful discernment. They are open to the opinions of others and to a vision that emerges from those places. While this is not natural for many, it can be learned. It is another essential ingredient necessary for shaping vision.

Lead...with Prophetic Vision Casting

Many clergy find the idea of prophetic leadership particularly appealing. While the nurturing pastor had been the predominant image for many in previous generations, the last decades have witnessed the emergence of a desire to lead a congregation through deep change into the promised land of new ministry. It is a coveted image captured in many pastoral conversations. We long to be leaders who serve as visionary catalysts, stimulating the prophetic imagination of a congregation into increased ministry development and growth.

Some leadership researchers in the business world promote this concept of visionary leadership. They affirm great leaders are successful in their vision casting. Effective leaders articulate compelling visions about the purposes of their organizations, capturing the imagination of the people they are called to lead.

Visionary leaders assist others to understand what they should be involved with and why what they do is important. They inspire people to accept responsibility for the implementation of the vision and resource them as they develop measurement of excellence. They recognize the limits and realities of their organization. As a result, they define their goals for excellence within those limits. They articulate a vision that empowers people, helping them understand how their efforts contribute to the vision.

James Macgregor Burns calls these people "transforming leaders."[21] He realizes that leadership not only makes a difference in the organization, but also elicits growth and maturity in the people they are leading. He believes that leadership should raise the vision, the beliefs, and the aspirations of the follower to a new level. Leaders will also shape new sets of values. They do so by articulating, reinforcing, and renewing the values of the organization because of their deep desire to see members mature and grow.

Effective leadership transforms people, inviting them to become more than they are today. It encourages value formation, meaning and even passion to the task. In all they do, effective leaders attempt to embed values and beliefs in the life and rhythm of the congregation so that behaviors of the members reflect the values they articulate. Leadership desires transformation and renewal.

Paul compares this prophetic leadership role to the encouragement of a father (1 Thess. 2:11–12). This wonderful metaphor is framed in three positional themes: urging, pleading, and encouraging. These three themes represent positions that effective leaders take at different times in the transformational process of vision casting for ministry.

Prophetic leadership, at times, moves out ahead of the congregation, "pleading" for renewed imagination for what might be for the church. Other times these leaders "urge" from behind pushing people along in the missional journey. At some point they will come alongside and "encourage" people to move deeper in their discipleship and their lives together as a community of faith. They empower congregations by delegating appropriate authority at different stages of life in the congregation while at the same time resourcing the possibilities so that others thrive in the tasks set before them.

Lead...from Influence

It is fascinating that Paul positions his discussion on encouragement at the end of his apology of his ministry among the Thessalonians. Paul appears to understand that prophetic, visionary leaders are able to encourage people to something more only because they have lived deeply a committed character of secured formational identity, gentleness of spirit, kindness, and sensitive humility.

Leaders will never be secure enough to encourage others to become something more if they are fearful of being discovered. They will never take risks if, because of hidden traits, they are fearful of being found out. Leaders, desperate for the praise of others, will play to the crowd and shape their ministry to elicit affirmation rather than to encourage prophetic imagination. They have too much to lose.

A friend discovered this in his ministry. He served as one of the most effective leaders in our tribe of churches in Canada. His leadership was bold and courageous but years of living in the shadows could not help but affect things he did. His character and his passion always seemed to be on edge, and his life was played close to the vest because he was fearful of being discovered, or simply ashamed of the hiddenness he had chosen. To be a friend was to be a sparring partner, ducking and weaving as he let you in close for a moment and then swiftly pushing you away with verbal and often caustic jabs. It was worth it, but friendship with him was tiring. He was still very effective, but we often talk about what difference a life more genuinely and deeply lived now makes in his leadership. It makes a difference in our friendship as well.

Lead...in Order to Model the Faith

This is by no means a new concept. Leaders have always brought themselves to the task. It is an inescapable reality that Paul describes well as he speaks once again to the Thessalonians. Reflecting on his own ministry among them, he points out at the beginning of his letter a crucial observation. He writes, "And you became imitators of us and of the Lord" (1 Thess. 1:6).

The implication of this statement is foundational. Paul realized people imitate or absorb the character of their leaders. He understood that leadership is a question of character and substance long before it is a question of technique or skill. Fundamentally, the core question of leadership from a theological framework is, "What do you want to imitate?" And the corollary question will be, "What will you celebrate?" The answers to these questions reveal a leader's values and measurements of effectiveness. Clergy working from a sense of self-awareness intentionally develop personal core values and characteristics that portray the kind of communities of faith they are called to form. Leaders must model these characteristics before they are ever incarnated into congregational life.

I am writing this chapter while in Kenya attending the funeral of one of the greatest leaders I have ever known. His name is Bishop Nathan Ngala and he served as the Bishop of the Africa Brotherhood Church (ABC) for sixty years. This indigenous body of churches numbering over a million and a half people stretches from Kenya to Rwanda, Uganda to Tanzania. He died this week at 110 years of age and I was given the privilege to attend and to speak at his funeral. I would gladly fly around the world out of respect for this great man.

The story of the development of the ABC is significant. Years ago, a group of young Kenyan leaders emerged out of the mission agencies of the time because of a radical belief that scripture meant what it said. They created an independent church based on the idea that the churches should be a people who cross tribal barriers, are self-sustaining in their ministry, and are self-governing in their leadership. In many ways, they were the emerging church of the 1940s in colonial Kenya, asking fundamental questions as to what the church should be.

Unfortunately, independent and indigenous churches are often overlooked in the life of established Christian church life in Kenya. However, this reality did allow them to mature without interruptions from the outside. This church has an integral ministry of evangelism and community development second to none in the country of Kenya and, I believe, in all of Africa. Every pastor and evangelist is taught leadership, evangelism, pastoral skills, and community development concepts, so that when they move into ministry their approach will be integrated and holistic. The ABC helps us model and train leaders for other churches in other countries.

Bishop Ngala's leadership character is modeled throughout the church. It is second nature to others in the church now because they became "imitators" of him and of Christ Jesus. When you ask why this church does not have issues around dependence to outside organizations, you cannot avoid the fact that the one who led them for so many years modeled mutuality and covenant partnership. After a visit to Canada to be among our churches, he returned to Kenya and immediately sent back some funds to cover the expenses of his trip. Recently, we invited one of their leaders to attend the World Aids Conference in Toronto and to speak in some of our churches. Bishop Ngala, in a public meeting, commissioned this young leader with these words, "If you ask for or take any money from Canadians, do not return." This great man's core values about self-sustainability and effective ministry are woven through this strong and vibrant church.

His character and leadership has built strong roots. Pride in their congregational life has translated into a remarkable ability to transition into new forms of self-determining governance. This is a remarkable testimony to Bishop Ngala's integrity and character in leadership.

All the literature on leadership points to the idea that leaders shape values and mobilize people through character, not just through technique and efficient management frameworks. Efficiency and technique may create good processes and systems, but they do not build deep communities of faith that effectively move into the borderlands of mission and ministry.

Leaders make ripples like stones thrown into a large pool of water, and these ripples affect the life of the church and its people in ever-widening circles. They create waves of movement that affect the mood, atmosphere, and vibrancy in the congregation. Most importantly, they shape the missional "IQ" and intent of the church they lead.

***Lead*...into the Community**

Borderland churches need borderland-friendly clergy, comfortable in the worlds they so passionately and purposefully encourage people to engage. Leaders wired only for Christian subcultures find it difficult to encourage borderland living because it is impossible to guide others to places of effective missionary engagement where you are not willing to go yourself.

Borderland living requires modeling by catalytic leaders. Charles Van Engen writes, "Merely developing authority–only telling what they should do and devising programs to do it, will not be enough to mobilize the people of God. The people must be shown a model that presses them to want to achieve those intentionally missionary goals of the congregation."[22]

Borderland leaders passionately desire to make community connections and are perceived by that context as community people able to relate genuinely. They study the rhythms, language, and faces of the community so that they accurately reflect the features of the culture in which they and their neighbors are enmeshed. As a consequence, they aid church members to reflect accurately about their local culture theologically. Theology allows borderland churches to incarnate and suggest alternatives.

If the *raison d'être* of the church is to move intentionally out into the community, their community awareness enables them to encourage and explore relevant methods of intentional encounter. Leaders make it possible. Lay and clergy leaders uncomfortable with this movement, however, will hinder any intuitive missional movements by congregations or even individuals. Borderland-unfriendly leaders paralyze congregations and stifle creativity in their desire to continue an emphasis on activity *inside* of the church. Their blindness to the worlds of engagement *outside* causes them to shape superficial and general observations of borderland people because ignorance and lack of lived experience breeds superficiality and generalizations.

Seeing their leaders willing and able to thrive in the borderlands is empowering. When congregations see leaders authentically relating to their cultural contexts, they attempt the same. Alan Roxburgh and Fred Romanuk, and others who write about missional church life, reflect a new expectation. They point out that in this new world of pastoral ministry:

> Discipling and equipping require a leadership that demonstrates encounter with the culture in action. In days ahead, the gown of the scholar must be replaced with the shoes of the apostle. This is not to diminish the importance of intellectual engagement, but it is a call for a shift of paradigm towards contextual engagement with the culture.[23]

The question of course is, "How?" The answer, however, is not as difficult as we think. Maybe we just do what Jesus did. He hung out with borderland people. In fact, he was criticized for doing so.

The religious establishment was incensed, but he spent time with those people anyway.

Leaders help communities to revise congregational possibilities into missional attitudes and relationships. They model it and, united with others, they shape the life of the congregation in the purposeful attempt of engaging the worlds outside the walls of their church.

Facing the Call of Borderland Leading

Who we are and who we see ourselves to be is crucial as leaders. We bring ourselves, our coping skills, relational ability, approach to faith, values, and even our sense of worth to leadership roles. If leadership is about creating a ripple effect, then the leader must ask what kind of ripples they want to create. We must ask the question posed earlier, "What do we want to imitate?"

In discussion with pastoral leaders effectively moving into the borderlands, some common themes emerge. These themes involve not yet attained qualities, but destinations and formational paths we must take. They are not held in balance or equally lived out, but often are held in great tension, creating thoughtful and intentional living. I have come to frame them with common images we have often used for leadership. The call of leadership today is a call to be *apprentice-pastor-theologian-missionary.*

Apprentice: Nurturing a Passionate Life in Jesus Christ

Dallas Willard reflects on this theme not just from the framework of being a leader, but also a disciple. He writes:

> As Jesus' disciple, I am his apprentice in kingdom living. I am learning from him how to lead my life in the Kingdom of the Heavens as he would lead my life if he were I. It is my faith in him that led me to become his disciple. My confidence in him simply means that I believe that he is right about everything: all that he is and says shows what life is at its best, what it was intended by God to be. "In him was life and the life was the light of men" (Jn. 1:4 NAS).[24]

It begins and ends here–living with Jesus in such a way so that all the aspects of my life are touched by what he calls me to be and do. Passionate followers of Jesus Christ are not born. They are forged in the hard disciplines of prayer, study, and reflective action.

All of our institutional organizations of Christianity must be focused on this possibility. If our youth ministries, congregational life, and seminary training do not produce passionate followers of Jesus

Christ, then we have failed in the formation of relevant leaders for the church of the twenty-first century.

These leaders nurture the formation of people who do not simply believe in Jesus but believe the things that Jesus believed in and seek to live out those beliefs in the light of all that they implicate.

> The crucial thing is that, as disciples, we have a plan for implementing the decision we have made to devote ourselves to becoming like our Master and Lord–to increasingly live in the character and power of Christ. Disciples are those who, seriously intending to become like Jesus from the inside out, systematically and progressively rearrange their affairs to that end, under the guidance of the Word and the Spirit. That is how the disciple lives.[25]

Pastor: Committed to the Formation of a Genuine Community of Faith

Borderland leaders understand that the primary task of a gathered church is to fling itself missionally into the world. Anything less is inadequate and produces navel-gazing pastoral leaders and stale nominalistic ineffectiveness in the church. The ideas of community building within the church and engaging the community of relationships and systems outside of the church have often been perceived as mutually exclusive.

The result is clergy leaders focused on one theme and not the other. Congregations that emphasize the former nurture a sense of being together in a kind of fellowship of the faithful without testing it in the gristmill of encounter with the worlds around them. The latter produces individualistic and detached activity, void of reference points for formational transformation.

Pastors are church people who believe that the developing of body life is critical for social action and evangelism. They love their people and tenaciously work to develop skills, attitudes, and atmospheres required not just to cast vision but to gather and empower people in the implementation of their missional vision. Leaders shape the community to become a place where genuine transparent and authentic relationship can take place. They do so in the belief that, without a community of faith, they are impotent in the missional task.

Missionary: Committed to Engaged and Incarnational Living Outside the Church

The missionary call is to understand the worlds we live in. Borderland leaders dialogue with places and people so that the skills required for effective engagement of the culture modeled by Jesus will take place in the lives of the people they serve. Pastors must understand the times in which they live, developing in themselves and others an ability to navigate and negotiate the complexities encountered.

Not unlike the missionaries of the past who traveled to far away places and were required to learn the languages, patterns, and values of the people they were seeking to engage, the missionary leaders today must do the same. Their motivation is sensitive, relevant, and intentional engagement with the culture. The result is genuine encounter.

Theologian: Committed to Live Deeply in the Questions

The role of theology has been suppressed in the last decades because of our love for the pragmatic and technique-oriented leadership of managerial missiology. Knowing the how-to of ministry replaced the tough and rigorous work of theological reflection. We worshiped at the altar of programmatic implementation, and its "god" often created ineffective incarnational living in the borderlands. Pragmatic planning is not wrong; it is simply not enough.

A deep theological and biblical reflective frame must be formed in the pastor's life. Pragmatic business models helpful in implementation do not necessarily produce deep churches and are wholly inadequate for the complexities of the times that we are in. Leaders cannot simply "have" a theology, they must learn to "do" theology, thoughtfully engaging in the task of cultural and relational interpretation through the lens of biblical reflection.

The tension of the first themes of apprentice-pastor-missionary is informed by this practice of theological reflection. When absent, the content required for deep effective discipleship formation, congregational development, and borderland engagement is absent as well. Hjalmarson challenges us to be a new kind of leader, one that is more organic and less organizational. He says: "We need a new kind of leader unconcerned about issues of marketing and structural maintenance and focused instead on discipleship and transformation, faithfulness, brotherhood and authenticity. We need leaders who are willing to step down in the world."[26]

The Challenge Ahead

It takes enormous courage to lead in this time. New metaphors and images are not just faddish suggestions but necessary reimaging of ancient leadership possibilities. They will enable formations of communities much different than those highlighted in the recent past.

Ultimately, these communities define themselves not by what they do in church activities on Sunday and midweek programs but by the production of transformed followers of Jesus Christ who live in the borderlands set before them.

Neighborhoods become places of relationship and not simply contexts for ministry. Relationships in the workplace are perceived to be places of genuine encounter. The call to gather together on Sunday for spiritual formation produces transformational possibilities in borderland living. Peter Senge puts it well:

> Poised at the millennium, we confront two critical challenges: how to address deep problems for which hierarchical leadership alone is insufficient and how to harness the intelligence and spirit of people at all levels of an organization to continually build and share knowledge. Our responses may lead us, ironically, to a future based on more ancient–and more natural–ways of organizing: communities of diverse and effective leaders who empower their organizations to learn with head, heart, and hand.[27]

A REST STOP ALONG THE WAY

- Identify what is "unique" and what is "normal" in the following aspects of the career situations of those who are part of your discussion group: transition, holidays, taxes, family time, reimbursable expenses, etc. Is the position of clergy all that unique? How? What are the implications?
- How do you as clergy leader handle the reality of irrelevance? What about the ambiguity of expectations? Where are you grounded? What does your "multifacetedness" look like?
- Who are the leaders you desire to imitate? Why?
- Take the time to reflect on your characteristics of transparency, humility, and sensitivity.
- What do you want to model for others?

5

Herding Cats

Leading a Church into the Borderlands

BORDERLAND COMPASS POINT

Cats are extremely difficult animals to direct. They require a unique kind of leadership. Just like cats, today's congregations require leaders who can infuse a particular atmosphere, whose style fits the context of their borderland, who are committed to the members and who can identify and renovate the constructs inherent in the congregations' life together. Leaders are offered some suggestions as well as alerted to both some potential obstacles and affirming markers.

It is one of my favorite television commercials. Western music plays quietly in the background as you are introduced to rough and tumble cowboys out on the range leading cattle across the broad expanse of prairie landscape. They speak lovingly of the activity in which they are involved and the mystery of its call. All of a sudden you realize that it is not cattle they are herding. These are not your ordinary everyday ranching cowboys. Their herd is a menagerie of long and shorthaired, Siamese and calico cats.

"There is no job like it," these weathered cowboys sneezing allergically tell us. They nurse the cuts and bruises, evidence of having moved these cats in the same direction to a common place. The commercial is actually about information technology at Vanderbilt University, but it serves as a great illustration for clergy leadership in the twenty-first century. "When you get them all to town at the same time, you know you have done a good job."

This is a video clip that, when shown at pastors' conferences, quite often elicits great laughter of knowing affirmation. There is no doubt in their minds that this is what it feels like to work as clergy leaders today. They know it because they have the emotional cuts and scrapes to prove it.

Atmosphere: The Art of Leading Cats

The image of herding cats captures the atmosphere and focus of contemporary leadership. The leadership roles of apprentice, pastor, missionary, and theologian require similar expressions to that of motivational herders–wooing, coaxing, and prodding people in the relative missional direction in which they believe they are called to go. They are no longer at the head of a pack willing to follow them anywhere with unequivocal loyalty. As Alan Roxburgh and Fred Romanuk write, "The key to innovating new life and mission in a congregation is not so much a strategy for growth as it is cultivation of people themselves."[1]

As a result, leadership is about atmosphere. Leaders serve as stimulators, nurturing a community of fellow travelers to follow Jesus into the borderlands of service and witness concerning the transformational nature of the gospel. If they are effective, leaders are able to cultivate an atmosphere of encouragement and nurture attitudes within the congregation that promote a missional imagination. People begin to dream dreams of mission that are not simply framed for growth but for community engagement.

It is good to remember that congregational "cats" come in an array of categories and levels of emotional stability. Good leaders know this. In truth, the varied temperaments, maturity, and experiences become an advantage to the community, empowering and enabling them to move in that same direction while, at the same time, giving permission for being at different places in that movement. Further, if people are allowed to be part of the decision-making process, the result is greater ownership for the vision.

Leaders shape values and keep the goals before the congregation in such a way that people are mobilized and transformed. They realize that program development and numerical growth may be important, but they serve as only one measurement for effectiveness in the church. Values appropriation and the implementation of vision that results in tangible transformation of people into engaged and embedded disciples becomes just as important a measurement. These leaders develop new sets of impact and effectiveness indicators framed around the theological themes necessary for effective borderland living. By casting vision and nurturing the values inherent in that purpose, leaders stimulate congregational action toward them.[2]

Cats follow leaders they trust and good leaders nurture that trust so that they can set the pace for the congregation both for change and for movement out into the world. The atmosphere of permission and experimentation helps to stimulate vision for the borderlands and guide people into exploring their missional journey. These attitudes allow congregations to navigate the white waters of change, which are necessary for moving from "come to" strategies to "go to" frames of ministry involvement.

The development of an atmosphere of encouragement, permission, and experimentation is one critical component in the leader's action plan toward borderland living. Other components are: demonstration of commitment, attention to context, and renovation of constructs. Each one deserves some intentional examination.

Commitment: Loving the Cats

Engaging a gifted young pastor in a spirited dialogue a few years ago made the need for a committed leadership very clear to me. He was describing his frustration with the small rural church he had recently come to lead. His presence in the church for only two years had borne little, if any, transformational fruit. His annoyance was expressed in the confident assurance that these people were not open to changes or worthy of his leadership. I listened as he spewed his frustration with indignant self-righteousness. Finally, I interrupted his diatribe with a question, "Do you plan to stay long?"

His look was incredulous. It was as if I had slapped him on the face with an obvious truth. "Of course not," he replied. "You know I grew up in the city. If a church in the city called me, I would take it in a heartbeat. Even if a call does not come, I will probably only stay three to four years."

This small rural congregation had come to accept that they would likely not ever be a pastor's first love. New seminary graduates would arrive itching to employ the latest ideas and church strategies, which, the congregation intuitively knew, were designed to make them more of a trendy urban-like congregation, one more like the pastor hoped to lead. For years, this congregation had provided a place of warmth and acceptance for youthful exuberant pastoral leaders desirous to experiment as they learned their ministerial craft. This congregation had learned through these years of church life that there were two constants–clergy came and clergy went. Young seminarians implemented their ideas with little sensitivity or commitment to longevity. These young leaders had no intention of sticking around to see their changes through.

Borderland leaders believe in the community of faith they are called to serve. They listen because they love their "cats." This is often ignored or neglected. Too often leaders fail to identify with, or sometimes even like, their people and their context. They certainly want the congregation to follow their leadership, but, tragically, they do not want to feel obligated to like them in the process. Martin Luther King was right when he said, "Whom you would change, you must first love."[3]

Context: Eliciting Style and Direction

Understanding the contextual nature of leadership is critical. It seems to go against our inclinations to consider that leadership is not primarily a natural gift mix formula. Leadership is giftedness in context. It requires a willingness on the part of the clergy leader to express his or her gifts in a style appropriate to the congregation.

Some leadership styles are inappropriate for a particular congregational expression while others are congruent. If leaders are unable to adapt to the context they are serving, they will certainly struggle. If they are unwilling to adapt, they will encounter constant resistance and be unable to create the attitudinal and atmospheric qualities necessary for the church to make the shift to borderland engagement. Leaders unwilling or unaware of the need to adapt to contextual realities reveal not only a stubbornness concerning themselves, but also a lack of commitment to the transformational changes they espouse.

For years, a mid-size neighborhood church filtered a succession of pastors. Each pastor entered his or her ministry with great hope and expectation. In each case, the congregation grew for a time, attracting several residents who were intrigued with the "new guy." The curiosity only lasted for so long, and soon after the change in leadership, the congregation would stagnate. The decision by each pastor had been the same–to move the congregation into a regional church framework, one that would expand its purview from the immediate neighborhood to a citywide focus. The result was a succession of pastors who lived through the same frustrating narrative.

A wall of resistance was encountered when the presentation of building plans clashed with the ethos of the people who made up the congregation. Proposed programs were rejected and eventually the pastor left in frustration over the perceived unwillingness of the congregation to move beyond its seemingly insular mind-set.

However, these people were not resistant to growth at all. Their hesitancy was toward the perceived impact of a congregational strategy that would move them from a parish framework to a more regional "drive to" church. Their church community was part of an older suburb, perceived as the perfect place to raise children. The people who made up the congregation had great longevity and credibility in the neighborhood. Successive generations moved back into the same neighborhood because of the warm and inviting place it was. Grown children repeated the cycle, moving back into the neighborhood with their young families. Renovations and additions to existing houses in this trendy residential area were perceived a better option than moving out into the larger homes of newer suburbs. This was an established neighborhood with a particular reputation. And congregants were fully involved in its activities.

Conversations with former pastoral leaders brought fascinating insights. One former pastor provided a stark stare of incomprehension to the rhythmic behaviors so obviously inherent in this congregation he once served. This was a church absolutely committed to a parish mentality and, in his seven years of ministry among them, he failed to comprehend how deeply this identity shaped their vision of themselves and their possibilities. This reality had shaped their contextual understanding of neighborhood and their life together as a church. They were neither anti-growth, nor resistant to change. They were simply unable to envision regionalization of their church because they were intelligent enough to understand that it would not be consistent with the life rhythms of the residents and that it would divert the focus of the church from the place that mattered to them the most, their neighborhood.

Finally, a pastor arrived who both understood the congregation and the community around it. He was someone who had been living in the community, who understood its rhythms, and who loved its blended complexity of people and community life. Together, pastor and people allowed the rhythms of the community to infiltrate the church. They became a "church for the neighborhood." Church program schedules accommodated neighborhood program schedules. Church members were encouraged to participate in neighborhood activities as service and ministry. The church building was opened up for community activities. The beliefs already at work in the congregation were understood as missional living. The leader who accepted this congruence of neighborhood and people set the congregation loose to be all they had hoped to be, having been given the permission to live it out.

Contextual leadership is sensitive leadership. It holds a tension between respect for the way things are and vision for the way things could be. The goal is always the same because the "the mission of the church since the time of Christ is to embody this reconciled community and invite others to be reconciled and renewed by joining the community."[4]

Constructs: Understanding Congregational Culture

Every congregation is distinct. Each is uniquely shaped by its experiences, its beliefs and values, and its communal story. The denominational heritage, if it has one, and the local history of the place in which it is situated have impacted both its ministry expression and its congregational dynamic. The tensions it has faced and processed as a congregation has built a story that is woven into the church and its life together. In fact, congregations are constructed cultures, which contain habits and rituals that shape the space in which they live and how they see themselves. While they may not always make sense to the observer, these rhythms are accepted and understood by the people who are part of them. Knowing them is what makes members feel like they belong.

Over time, congregations develop values (what is accepted as best), choreography (how one should behave and act), and even a unique language (how groups distinguish themselves in communication from others) that are distinctly theirs as a community. Every congregation weaves together threads of history, rhythms, and rituals that elicit the recurring cultural practices as a church community. Often only long-standing members truly understand all these unwritten rules at their deepest levels.

It was one of those Sundays when a sacred convergence took place. I could sense that the congregation was alive with the presence of God, as even the sermon appeared to capture the people in hushed attentiveness. Moved by the moment and open to the possibilities of response by the people, I invited people to respond in a faithful stepping out from the pews and coming to the front for prayer. My tradition had always called this the "altar call," but, in my desire to be relevant and sensitive to the many in our congregation who were not from a churched culture, I simply invited them to respond if they wished to take faith in Christ seriously. I told them that if they wished to symbolize the choice they had made that day to take a new spiritual path centered on Jesus, then they could come down to the front as we sang the last song and members of the pastoral staff would be available to pray with them.

The song was sung with hushed anticipation. But while the sacred moment continued, no one was moved to come forward. Somewhat disappointed, I offered the benediction and then proceeded to the back of the church to shake hands at the door. Almost immediately, I was accosted by a young couple who had been attending the church as an initial foray into exploring their spiritual journey within a church setting. They had walked into this old church at the center of the city and, over the previous few months, tentatively begun to dig deeper by cultivating a new spiritual sensitivity within a Christian framework.

She appeared extremely agitated as she thrust her face close to mine and blurted out a blunt but pointed question, "What the hell did you want us to do?" I confess to being flustered both by her intensity and by the choice of the words she spoke at the door that day. Shocked, I could only blurt out a defensive, "Excuse me?"

She said it again with even greater force, "What the hell did you want us to do?" I am someone who has not been isolated from such expletives, but this, I knew, was far too much for the institutionally alert religious people waiting in line to shake my hand. These were words never spoken before at the door of this great cathedral church and so, with a great sense of damage control, I moved them quickly away to a quieter area far from the entry way and the pharisaical attitudes of the religious establishment, hoping that these stunning words had gone unnoticed.

Her intense questioning continued as I sought for clarification concerning the question she posed. Her response slapped me in the face. She said, "You said something about taking our spiritual journey seriously, about looking at Jesus as a person with whom we could trust our lives. Well, I thought it was time to do just that and I looked at my husband and told him that maybe we should take Jesus seriously and he agreed. The problem is that we didn't know what the hell we were supposed to do." She left me with a priceless suggestion that I have never forgotten. "Gary, the next time you offer such an invitation, you damn well better give clearer instructions." I have ever since.

The unique themes and unwritten rules are known as *constructs*. They exist in every community of people. They have an amazing potential to become mine fields of resistance and pitfalls of embarrassment for those leaders who come to a church from outside the culture. Taking them for granted will only prove frustrating. Ignoring them will only strengthen the resistance that takes place around vision casting for a different future. Identifying them enables congregational leaders to comprehend both the limitations of the congregation and the realistic possibilities set before them. Understanding them will directly impact the ability to create transformation and to achieve strategic outcomes. Renovating them is critical for the leader's ability to persuade and move congregations to imagine a borderland direction.

Recently a friend serving in a historical cathedral church described an encounter with a cultural construct in the congregation. In a desire to build bridges to the young emerging leadership in the congregation, the mission committee had designed a short-term mission experience that would allow for his participation in order to foster the development of trust between his pastoral leadership and these younger participants. When the idea arrived at the larger leadership council for approval, he was surprised by how quickly and adamantly it was rejected.

The rationale was very simple and seemed to border on the absurd. Participation in the mission experience would mean that he would be away on a Sunday. And, he was told, it is unacceptable for the senior pastor of the church to be away on a Sunday. He could, if he wished, go as part of his vacation but not as part of his work.

The cultural construct at work in this situation is obvious. The primary activity of the minister–in this case, the senior pastor of this church–is assumed to take place on Sunday. It is nonnegotiable within this congregational culture and it has numerous implications. It is a commonly held construct for "come to" churches and results in a propensity to focus all the major resources on the Sunday morning event. It will also result in modes of evaluation focused often on that one particular event–the worship service.

My friend's attempts to reason with the leaders of the congregation were fruitless. No rational argument could change their mind. In fact, it was not a rational problem at all. It was a cultural construct that made perfect sense to the people who were part of it and seemed nonsense to those from the outside. The senior pastor must be present on Sunday morning and, until a fundamental transformation takes place around the deeper constructs regarding the meaning and nature of the church–a renovation, if you will–this construct erects a roadblock to any activities that challenge the cultural norm. It is important to note that the leaders were not trying to be mean-spirited. In truth, they were defending their community's constructs.

Another way to grasp the meaning of *constructs* is to think of them in terms of the assumptions a congregation holds. Assumptions, as we all know, are very difficult to alter. They have been built up over a long period of time and they have been exercised within the life of the congregation to such an extent they can become almost impenetrable by outsiders. They serve as the unquestioned congregational mythology that wraps the congregation's view of itself and its internal workings. They shape the views about outsiders and even about outsiders who come to belong. Over time, they form the systemic psyche of the church, weaving an intricate web of rules that become automatic in how people respond out of them.

I once heard a story about an airplane company. It seems their latest model was simply too heavy. Engineers were sent back to the drawing board to find ways the weight could be reduced. One member of the design team bravely questioned the reason for needing steel frames in the headrests of the seats. They reviewed the research on safety but could find no reason for having steel frames in the head rests. They turned to the files on the history of the design and there discovered that the reason for putting steel frames in the head rests dates back to the old fighter planes of World War I. The steel frames protected the soldier sitting in front from wayward bullets of the solider sitting behind manning the machine gun. It had been years since anyone had questioned this assumption.

Assumptions are often lived out at a subconscious level. After a long period of time, they no longer require articulation by the faithful. Simple acquiescence is assumed. If they go unchallenged, the church becomes stuck, unable to change or move into new places of borderland engagement. Before they can be challenged, they must first be understood. They must be artfully coaxed out of the congregational subconscious and brought to the surface so that they can be discussed. Then and only then can their assumptive realities be challenged.

Coming to Know the *Context* and Beginning to Change the *Constructs*

Leaders have the best perspective from which to see the dynamics of congregational cultural constructs. If they are willing to take the time to observe and analyze, their patience will be rewarded. Behaviors are a mirror image of the congregational beliefs at work, revealing what members hope for in the church and even in their own lives. Through these various behaviors, it is possible to discover the dynamics that are of greatest influence in the congregation. Developing the skills to probe and to analyze best uncovers these congregational behaviors. By taking time to be with people through everyday living in and among the community, leaders will be able to discern which constructs are untouchable, which can remain without adverse effect on change, and which need renovation within the congregational culture.

I learned how important it is to understand before you confront in one of the most difficult times in my pastoral life. Having become stuck in a frozen place of assumptions, I faced the saints of the church that I had come to serve. Although they were telling me that they wanted to change, these faithful and wonderful people still held to the conviction that things should stay the same. The church had been in a steady decline for more than twenty-five years but they still held to the belief that all that was required was to do what they had always done, just better. My role was to be winsome enough from the pulpit and then people would come.

This was, of course, ridiculous. The issues were much deeper than a change of pastors. Many members had led years of rigid and lifeless faith. Many activities of church life were no longer relevant to the people they so desperately wanted to enter their sanctuary. The forms and rhythms were no longer replicable realities, and the worse part of it was the impact that had on their children.

Many of them had watched as their children drifted away from church over the years, either to other churches or from any church involvement at all. They grieved those losses but had never connected the dots to anything that they had done as a congregation. It was always someone's fault–a former pastor or some unfortunate sociological incident that affected their life as a congregation. They were convinced that their decline was totally disconnected from the approach they took toward life in the church.

Deep down they knew the truth, but they did not want to face its implications. They knew that things needed to change, but they were frightened–not so much of the change itself, but about what would happen if it did not work. The question was painful but strategically critical. Looking at them with the compassionate understanding of hours spent in conversations about the church and their families, I asked them the question they did not want to discuss, "Where are your children?"

They were stung with the question and a silence fell over the group. I then went on to say that this is the crucial and important question that must be asked because it strikes at the root of the problem. If things are acceptable and as good as they thought, then why could they not reproduce that excitement in their children? "Why have your children left?"

The discussion that ensued that night was a sacred time filled with moments of tears and painful words. These wonderful people broke out of the unexamined and unquestioned constructs from which they had lived for too many years as a congregation. They dealt with the hard question, many of them for the first time. Unknowingly, as they were challenging these assumptive beliefs, they also were beginning to look at what might need to happen differently.

Listen...for What Is Really Important

Pastoral leadership does not occur in a vacuum; it is deeply rooted in community. It is a theological reality critical for contemporary culture and essential for leading change. God created us for community and God placed the new covenant in the context of the community of faith–the church to be lived out into the world.

To think that you will be able to clarify and empower the missional vocation of the church by wise strategic decision-making is folly. It will take much more than that. It will require a communal leadership approach that lives deeply into the congregation both listening and seeking to understand. Only then will leaders be able to comprehend the shape of the vision possible through the congregation and its congruency with the context in which they are placed.

Active communal listening ensures that the shaping of congregational life is not simply a solitary act perpetrated by clergy leaders on the church. Most congregations grow suspicious of leaders who only push their own ideas or, even worse, franchise the ideas of others. People take seriously leaders who take them seriously. A sign hanging in a trauma and reconciliation office in Rwanda struck a colleague of mine. On the sign is written these words, "Listening is the greatest act of love."

Listening cultivates healthy diversity within congregational life and affirms its presence as a shared core value. If diversity is unappreciated, threatening dysfunction, needless conflict and relational tension ensue. When listening refines community, life in community is less threatening. Opinions are welcomed. Visions become larger because they are a shared reality. Congregational listening based on an atmosphere of trust provides a critical condition from which missional engagement can take place by matching the congregational possibilities (discerned through the listening process) with the borderland potentials (discerned by engaging the community around the church and natural networks of relationships of each congregational member).

The life and teachings of Jesus provide a model for how listening changes things. Jesus listens intently, assessing the differing needs and concerns of individuals and hearing the deepest places of their hearts.

Communal listening is critical in international work. The issues and needs of the so-called developing world appear obvious through cursory observation. This is especially so for those of us who come from the global North, where solutions are at the core of our response. Too often, without patient and careful listening for the deeper issues at work, we move too swiftly toward solutions that prove to be flawed.

North Americans witness the plight of vulnerable children orphaned through the pandemic of HIV/AIDS in Africa and they are moved by what they see. They, however, do not take time to hear some of these children. It is easy to treat all orphaned children the same, for they all appear to have similar needs for supervision and parenting. The tragedy is that we have missed the uniqueness of their situations. Well-meaning North Americans provide what seems the obvious solution for all of the numerous parentless households–orphanages. However, for some orphans, this response is disastrous. Some of them are still living on the small subsistent farms left to them upon the death of their parents. If they are removed from this homestead, their claim to this ancestral land may be lost forever.

The orphanage response solves the problem, but the absence of intentional and compassionate listening results in an inability to grasp the deeper issues at work. When some of the orphans are removed from their homes, they lose their land to squatters and, at the same time, lose the extended family connections so critical to African life. For some, the crisis is extended and the problems amplified. The greater need is for contextual African solutions to emerge, solutions that will deal with the core needs as well as the strengths and resilience of the vulnerable children. These solutions will only be discerned through a process of deep and compassionate listening.

Learn...about the Constructs

How do you learn to observe and listen intently enough to discover the deeper constructs and issues at work in a congregation? It is not easy and it is not natural. Edgar Schein, a MIT Professor of Management and author of *Organizational Culture and Leadership: A Dynamic View,* contends that many of the problems confronting contemporary leaders can be traced to their inability to analyze and evaluate organizational cultures.[5] They try to implement new strategies, but soon discover that their strategies fail because they were unable to grasp the culture of the organization.

Many clergy experience the same reality. They come to their congregations with the anticipatory inner challenge to "shake the place up." Some even feel a sense of entitlement around the implementation of sweeping changes that they believe are so obviously needed by their new congregational charge. Facing this impatient and uninformed leadership attitude, congregations invariably resist, not because they do not see the need for change or even desire it, but because they intuitively sense that violence is about to take place around the cultural constructs that they hold as sacred and on which the church is built. They may need to change but they need to be first understood.

Change takes time. The deep transformational movement from the "come to" orientation of churches shaped in the twentieth century to "go to" churches so crucial in the twenty-first century will take time as well. Nothing will happen without a healthy respect and understanding of the congregational constructs at work in a particular congregation. Respect does not mean acceptance. It does, however, mean being aware of the power these factors hold in a church's life.

Discover...Intentionally Those Who Guard the Constructs

One straightforward way to discover the constructs of a congregation is by getting to know the keepers of the flame. They can be found in every church. Not surprisingly, they are usually a small group that has emerged over the years to serve as custodians of the community's constructed values and beliefs. Their ownership of these congregational assumptions is held in a way that no other group can and they take their stewardship seriously.

These custodians are critical in any transformation process. Gaining their trust is often difficult because of the power they hold in the congregation and the unwavering sense that they are right in the convictions they steward. This reality makes them a formidable force to encounter. They may be well-intended in their custodial role, but they are potentially dangerous resisters.

In a small urban congregation, one faithful family serves as custodians of the constructs. They actually oppress the congregation with their beliefs. Opposing points of view are not allowed because this family is absolutely committed to the idea that there is no other way to see things. They would be appalled to think that some people in the congregation feel bullied in their conversations with them. After all, the family wants only what is best for the church.

The assumptions they steward are well articulated but they are also unexamined in the light of the changes in the neighborhood and culture around them. It is as though they were built for a time and a place that no longer exists.

This family has faced off with a succession of pastors and lay leaders over the years, holding to their sacred assumptions. Each of these leaders attempted to confront the dissonance between the culture of the congregation and the challenges of the world around. Several even saw some success, but all experienced the brunt of passionately spoken words of resistance encased in scriptural references used as proof of their position. Those words have a way of creating an atmosphere of exclusion.

Custodial holders of the flame do not need to function on official boards, because their authority is often informal. Pastoral and emerging lay leaders interested in new possibilities absorb the brunt of criticism through continuous subtle confrontations. The power to resist is an assumed entitlement by the sub-group; nobody has granted it, but, then again, nobody has successfully challenged them either.

Congregational members, fearful of confrontation, allow the dysfunctional behavior to continue. They are just afraid. The result is that people eventually just drift away.

Smaller congregations are more susceptible to this custodial oppression. Large congregations have their own set of problems, but the smaller congregations are more accessible to the entrapment of an oppressive hold by a group's custodial behavior over congregational life. Afraid of conflict and tension, unwilling to confront or support those who would, they become a church ruled by a few and frustrating to many.

Congregational constructs express preferences for certain behaviors or certain outcomes. They are the norms that set out the behaviors accepted by others and the culturally acceptable ways of pursuing goals. They have an amazing resilience. If leadership lacks the courage or the patience to challenge these constructs, then vision and hopes for a better future are pipe dream fantasies.

*Challenge...*Destructive Constructs

If leaders are to serve as catalysts for transformation and reimagine a new way, they will need to alter the conditions and constructs that are holding the congregation back. They must challenge the people they serve to radically reimage their assumptions, reinterpret their beliefs, and reframe their values, developing a process that establishes a new set of constructs from which borderland existence can emerge.

Destructive constructs are often embedded in the ways congregations do their business. Over the years, a congregation I served had come to pride itself in its perceived parliamentary efficiency. Minutes were exact. Chairmanship bordered on dictatorial. Protocol was policed. The result was that only those who knew the rules and were sufficiently confident to speak within them had a say in congregational decision-making. As newer members started serving in leadership positions on the council, they were intimidated by the dominance of long-standing members whether or not these members held any official church office.

We had to discover a way to foster more involvement and to encourage more dialogue. The risk was huge. We arranged the chairs in small circles rather than leaving them in the typical auditorium form. We set the Chair's microphone in the middle of the room. As members came into the hall, they were given a nametag with a particular color signifying which conversational circle they were to join. The agenda indicated three key issues to which the church leadership wanted the congregations input. Each issue was introduced by the chair, who then gave time for conversation to take place in the circles. Each circle reported the key points of their discussion. After every circle was heard, a vote was called. While the few previously dominating members felt they had not been given enough floor time, other long-standing members had been given voice in the decision-making process for the very first time. Challenging this construct in the life of our congregation served as a turning point in our journey together.

Coax...out the Missional Desire

Borderland leaders come with the expressed hope of aiding their community of faith to live faithfully into the network of neighborhoods and relationships. Without understanding the constructs that are at work preventing their congregations to move toward these new possibilities, leaders will unwittingly collide with congregational cultures and continue to be surprised by reactions that appear out of scope with respect to the suggested vision possibilities.

Innocent or naïve clergy leaders who arrive at the church with a misguided assumption of bringing truth rather than hope to them may actually miss the possibility that a healthy sense of mission might already exist within the congregation. They may only need to tap into it. The congregation, for example, may have a profound sense of the gospel and its call on their lives. It may be deeply embedded within the congregational culture but never been allowed to be brought to the surface. Coaxing and nurturing its emergence will unlock a latent missional vision.

Leaders too often assume that the missional imagination is absent within the congregation. Our failure as leaders may be that we have ignored the healthy embedded narrative that resides in a congregation simply because we did not listen for it nor did we take the time to allow it to emerge. It might unlock the future, but it may not be the kind of future we want. These embedded narratives have the potential to become reasons for change.

Women's missionary societies are often an example of this. The missionary unions of women have been involved in ministry to refugees and immigrants. For many years, they funded inner-city ministry deemed unacceptable in the eyes of the established church and its leaders. They saw the missional vision of global ministry long before their male counterparts.

Women's missionary societies have a radical and revolutionary past. However, in too many cases they have lost their imagination and passion. The commitment to borderland living still resides in many of these faithful women. They have understood sacrificial missional living, but only within the particular framework in which it was expressed in the past. The framework may not be adequate for today's times, but the commitment still lies deep within them. Lost in the desire to capture younger women to their institutional agenda, members have forgotten what captured their own attention and passion in the past. It was not the program that captured them. It was the passionate missional desire to make a difference around the world and around their community.

The art of leadership is to develop the sensibilities and skills necessary to recognize and enable vision to emerge from within the congregation. It is to help people seek God where God is already at work. The web of personal relationships, their practices, sacred institutions, and accepted behaviors, if allowed to surface, are a deep reservoir of possibilities in the church. If cultivated, they can, in many cases, thrive.

Gathering the stories and seeking to understand them can be challenging. Transformation does not happen overnight. True change always takes time. David Bosch says that new paradigms do not establish themselves quickly. They take time to develop distinctive contours and often leaders find themselves "thinking and working in terms of two paradigms."[6] One is the paradigm of the gains that have been made in the transformational process while living with the tension of the realities that have not yet been altered. All of this takes place in the continuing act of communicating a reimagined future. The crisis of leadership is not that we lack a reimagined future. It is that we lack the courage to be patient enough to see it emerge over time.

Align...Rituals and Language

Every congregation has rituals that affirm their community constructs and enable church members to keep track of their history and even the purpose for their existence. They help define where they came from and who they are. As they are repeated, they add meaning, texture, and richness to congregational life. They are also foundational bases that make it possible to cope during challenging times of uncertainty. And, they create loyalty.

This truth became apparent to me one Christmas Eve at First Baptist. A number of people still called First Baptist their home church because of familial ties even though their attendance mostly focused on Christmas and Easter. One year our midnight Christmas Eve candlelight service attendance was overflowing and energy filled the sanctuary. One of these loyal part-timers spoke enthusiastically to me at the door after the service. "Gary, we are really growing aren't we? Isn't it exciting?" The Christmas Eve ritual anchored him even though he only entered the building twice a year.

Rituals can be discretionary. They may be performed by a single individual, by a group, or by the entire community, in arbitrary places or in places especially reserved for these rituals. They may be public or private. They may be restricted to a certain subset of the community or may enable or underscore an entire congregational frame. They welcome, affirm, confirm, and commission within the foundational frameworks at work in the congregation.

However, there can be a great dissonance between the ritualistic affirmations and the stated purpose of the church. Words of inclusion to seekers attending the church can be negated by structures and language that constantly remind seekers that they do not belong. Worship leaders may say to the congregation that all are welcome at whatever place they are in their journey of faith. But, when the leaders also say, "this is a song everyone ought to know," they are declaring that a certain level of knowledge is required. Language can neutralize ritual. Rituals and language must align.

Sadly, I find that many leaders act as if rituals are nonexistent. Many, in so-called contemporary churches, live in the illusionary idea that rituals only exist as part of the liturgical tradition of the church. Blind to the rituals and language at work in their congregations, they are unable to see how these rituals work against them. I am amazed, for instance, how often I discover churches whose music and dress code has been drastically altered, but whose rituals concerning inclusion and language strangely have remained intact. The worship they enter into has more "snap" in the expressed desire to create an atmosphere that is conducive to those who are unchurched, but their language and rituals are unaltered and remain inhibiting. Rituals hold power in congregations and, as a result, they must be brought into convergence with the overall revisioning process of the church. Only in the convergence of ritual and content will transformational change be possible.

An old First Church held a commissioning service on a Sunday in September. Volunteers working in the church programs that included ministry to children, music, boards, and committees were called forward for a ritual of commissioning. For a number of years, the content of the missional message from the preaching and teaching of the church declared that ministry took place outside the walls of the church as well as inside, that people's vocation in the workplace and neighborhoods in which God had placed them was ministry of the church. However, the commissioning service implied something profoundly different. It affirmed the value for those who worked within the traditional programs of church ministry and excluded those who sensed a call to vocation outside in their workplaces and neighborhoods.

Teachers in mid-week ministry to children were affirmed, but faithful teachers in the public school from Monday to Friday were missed. Participation on committees and councils within the church were recognized, while salt-and-light businesspeople went unnoticed. Subtly this yearly ritualistic affirmation presented a powerful message about what was really important and what was not. It told the congregation what faithful living looked like and it all happened in the church. It presented the belief that true Christian commitment expressed itself within the walls of the church.

Ironically, I had unknowingly participated in this ritualistic war that neutralized what I taught from the pulpit. My epiphany happened one Sunday when, in the middle of this commissioning ritual, I realized how destructive this exclusionary ritual really was. I was horrified. I paused for a moment of confessional flagellation concerning what I had missed for so many years. Turning to the congregation, I apologized for my blindness and spontaneously invited any who felt a specific sense of call to faithfully live as disciples of Christ in the places in which they worked and lived, to come forward and join the others for a prayer of commissioning. A coach of a boys' hockey team, a lawyer, and a baker were only some of those who came forward that day. For once, word and ritual came together in a synergistic whole and the moment was electric.

I have never forgotten that sacred moment because that day I learned about rituals and the potential they have to cultivate missional values and purpose. They fuel the possibilities and can, if used properly, expand the imagination of the people toward what they are called to be and do. They educate and inform people concerning what the church expects from its people as a community of gathered and sent people.

The Bible is a beautiful, subversive, religious, and even political document full of language rich in its description of a new hope for individual lives, relationships, and communities where justice, love, and peace will find a home. Rituals and words have the powerful ability to invite people to sing the new song and, at the same time, encourage them to live out into the new world of borderland challenge.

Being aware of the language we use in the community of faith is crucial if we are to assist others to live the borderland narrative, and we do so by telling the story of crossing over and calling it out from others. The language that we use must capture the imagination of people so they become captive to a glimpse of what God is doing in the church and in the community of neighborhoods and relational networks. Transformation is the goal–a transformation of values, attitude, and atmospheric conditions necessary for borderland churches to be effective. The story to be told is an adventure story, inviting people to journey as God's sent people into the "places where Christian faith, unfaith, and other faiths intersect." It is to evoke a personal commitment to borderland living.

Rituals and language nurture inclusiveness in ministry, enabling the church to model the radical new creation set out in scripture (2 Cor. 5). It reflects a rejection of divisions along socioeconomic lines, empowers women, and crosses multicultural boundaries, displaying the rich diversity found in this new reign of Christ. Inclusive ministries are not about being politically correct. They are about mirroring scripture's call for unleashing the full potential of deployed followers of Christ exercising the gifts they have been given.

***Build...*Authentic Structures**

Even cats need structure, but they do not always appreciate the need. In much of my dialogue with young leaders in the church, I hear a cry for structural change that often appears to be more of a reaction to past experiences. The proposed structural change appears more like knee-jerk reactions to bad experiences rather than clear strategic developments of structures to enable missional borderland living.

However, most present structures in congregations were developed in the same way. At a particular time, they were valid attempts to respond to the societal and cultural issues. They were a reaction to a particular need at a specific time. Issues change, however, except in the minds of those who believe that the previous structures now contain some sacred quality.

As conditions and circumstances change in culture, structures must change as well. They do so to meet the emerging implications these conditions have brought. If people carry a sacred commitment toward existing structures, especially around denominational governance or leadership styles, structural change will become a fascinating minefield of possible conflict. These conflicts will be accentuated if congregants live unaware and ignorant to the vast cultural and societal changes around them.

Alan Roxburgh and Fred Romanuk, in their book on missional leadership, insightfully unpack the challenge of both existing and changing views of structure.[7] They point out that old structures were invariably centralized, bureaucratic, and top-down structures that demanded blind loyalty. Change was designed to occur slowly and almost imperceptibly. As a result, institutions over time became increasingly more resistant to challenges.

Changes began to take place in society, and a growing sense of insecurity toward existing structures was a direct result. Movements of change were intensely resisted by organizations, which only threw cosmetic morsels to the movements of change in the desire to satisfy their hungry longings for something different. They understood that you earned your place of influence and found your authoritative voice only after many years of playing the organizational game that the present leaders had been previously forced to play.

Roxburgh makes this point:

> The dominant means whereby these new structures and institutions of modernity achieved this was through the development of the modern corporation, which became, as Henry Ford, GM and IBM so elegantly demonstrated, the primary institutional form of social structure for much of the 20th century. The modern corporation was built on hierarchies of organizational life, professionalization of all elements of work and social services, impersonal bureaucratization and a strategic planning process that could predict outcomes and results. It was a brilliant creation for the new, modern industrial society.[8]

In the twentieth century, churches of North America and Europe were a mirror reflection of the modern company, and many thrived using this model. Gradually change took place in culture and society and an incredible tension arose within many congregations as their structures began to become unwieldy and eventually fail. Since the old patterns of loyalty no longer worked, congregations began to feel the effects of a changing world.

Roxburgh calls this shift a movement from structure to anti-structure.[9] Putting it succinctly, many people no longer feel that they need to either play the game or even treat the structures as sacred, foundational, and nonnegotiable. They are willing to take on and put off structures that others may feel are written in stone. This does not mean that people are not looking for structure. It means they have become utilitarian, believing that structures should work, being efficient and not cumbersome.

If inadequate structures are no longer sacred, then they are to be held loosely. This especially becomes true for borderland churches for whom identity is found in the fulfillment of the missional purpose of the church. Leadership and authority in these types of churches is earned through trust-building relationships, and not granted by appointment to position. Consequently, people who continue to hold onto positions of leadership, assuming that the role brings with it granted authority, automatic respect, and blind loyalty will struggle in this new emerging community of faith.

I remember with great clarity a time in my own life where this clash of structural ownership took place. The denominational leaders had gathered a group of young pastors whom they considered the "mavericks" of our denomination. We were the young bucks wanting our say. We were overly confident and somewhat arrogant, but also no longer blindly loyal or, for that matter, especially respectful to positional authority figures. After a long discussion focused on changes that we felt needed to take place, one of the leaders, asking for patience, looked me in the eye and said, "Gary, I pastored and worked hard to attain this position in our denomination. I think I have earned your respect." It was an unfair request in the new world in which we were living. It begged for blind loyalty whether deserved or not. "No," I said, "you have earned the position, but you still have a long way to go to earn my respect."

Loosen...the Bureaucracy

If you can appreciate the great shifts that have taken place in structures and organizational systems, then you will understand that the need today is for structures that are flexible and nimble. Participants in congregational life will neither have the patience nor the willingness to commit to structures that are obviously restrictive and more focused on organizational survival than on mission. As Bill Easum says, "Today's fast pace of change renders bureaucracy helpless."[10]

The centralized frameworks of the past have been rendered obsolete by the information age of Internet and global media. Resources are more readily available and communication is instant in both its expectations and its accessibility. Relationships emerge out of many networks connected to multiple places of influence. Structures in the future need to promote networking possibilities. At the same time, structures must be open to innovation–to the trial and error of experimentation that is associated with flexibility and nimble ability to both make decisions quickly and to alter courses taken just as fast.

Jonathan Wilson places the challenge of nimble structures in perspective when he writes, "The strength of evangelicalism is its willingness to adapt its practices to the demands of Christian mission. Its weakness is its willingness to neglect our identity within the people of God… [D]emands of adaptation and faithfulness commits [*sic*] us to both."[11] The challenge to reimagine the church for this time is to ensure that structures facilitate a commitment to the gospel and to the grand purpose of a passionate missional focus.

Congregations need to act more as movements than institutions. Movements are more nimble because they hold overarching commitments, such as the mission of the church in the borderlands, aggressively. They are able to remain nimble by altering course quickly when changes are required. Movements make decisions in a fluid atmosphere foreign to the gridlock of bureaucratic processes so often found in church and denominational structures of today. For borderland movements, all that matters is the passionate purpose around why the church exists.

If organizational structures can no longer count on the blind loyalty of the past, the corresponding truth is that that loyalty can never be taken for granted. In the church, people must know that leaders are worthy of journeying with them in their missional task and, consequently, leaders are always actively nurturing trust and participation.

Effective leaders distinguish themselves by their ability to inspire followers to commit passionately to the cause anyway. They appear to be able to hold authority, power, and position lightly and do not take themselves as seriously as the task for which they seek to be a catalyst.

Ready for the Drive

I have suggested that herding the cats of today's congregations toward borderland living is a process of listening, learning, discovering, challenging, coaxing, aligning, building, and loosening. In addition, many helpful resources do an excellent job of creating tools for assessment for congregational health. Other books move beyond analysis and description to prescriptive steps toward a more hopeful congregational future.[12]

As with any journey, there is always the possibility of taking a wrong turn. I suggest leaders try to avoid some obstacles along the way toward borderland living. A brief description of each is warranted.

Try to avoid becoming *inwardly wired.* Inwardly wired churches only take counsel from themselves. They know what is best and outsiders are not allowed to speak into the life of their church unless they sound exactly like the members. Anne Lamott once said that you could tell when people have made God in their own image because he hates the things and people that they hate.[13] It may be only human to listen only to yourself, but it is not healthy or helpful.

Try to avoid being *outwardly oblivious.* Outwardly oblivious church members appear unwilling to face the real world. They are unable to grasp the deep crisis of change in society and, as a result, ignore the realities. Worse, they live in the naïve assumption that they will be able to return to the way it was. While change for change's sake is pointless, ignoring changing realities proves more destructive to congregations, especially if it is a way of blocking the reality of what needs to be transformed and changed in the church.

Recognize the current tendency toward *leadership aversion.* Perhaps this is more of a trend in Canada than in the United States. It is the tendency for congregations to want leaders and leadership structures to remain passive. Congregations today seem more comfortable when leaders stay inwardly focused around the care and nurture of the congregation itself.

Try to avoid *trivial pursuits.* This is clearly revealed in what the congregation believes is worth fighting about. When congregations begin to argue about the trivial and nonessentials rather than core issues of the gospel, they are unable to join in the missional adventure. Congregations caught in trivial arguments such as "whether or not they should sing choruses or hymns" or "whether or not the new flooring should be carpet or tile" will not be able to passionately dialogue about the great missional implications of the faith.

Try not to *ignore those on the edges.* I once heard a management consultant suggest that we ought to listen to people on the edge of organizations pushing into new areas of service. These "out on the edge" people are usually pointing the way that we need to go. How a church or a denomination deals with its mavericks says a lot about the health of the movement. Insecurity creates a sense of threat. If the institution cannot listen to those with whom they are uncomfortable, they will likely be unable to be sufficiently creative and courageous to move into the borderlands.

Try not to *fear evaluation.* Many congregations are gripped with the fear of evaluation. We seem to always take everything personally. Intuitively we may know that something needs to be changed, but we do not want to face it. Without sufficient and healthy feedback, our effectiveness and accountability falter.

Resist *nominalistic passion.* This church pathology was introduced as John wrote to the church of Laodicea (Rev. 3:16). It is a fact that some of us have become lukewarm in our spirituality.

Leaders can be assured they are moving in the right direction when they avoid these obstacles. And, they can be assured they are moving in the right direction when they encounter certain key markers. I recommend that leaders pay attention for the following affirmations.

- Be alert to an *anticipatory atmosphere.* Recognize when members in the congregation start expressing a belief that they are part of a movement and that what they are doing is making a difference.
- Celebrate demonstrations of *caring fellowship.* When positive attention is called to that which is taken for granted, momentum toward a supportive environment is fostered.
- Recognize *faithful connectedness.* Search out those members who are making connections between their professed and their practiced faith.
- Affirm *dynamic spirituality.* The desire to explore and engage in regular and meaningful spiritual disciplines is an indicator of moving in the right direction.
- Recognize *engaged living.* Attend to and join the relationships and activities that congregational members have and do in their neighborhoods and workplaces.
- Celebrate *sacrificial generosity.* When members give something that costs them something, be it time or resources, recognize it as a sign of spiritual maturity and deep commitment.
- Accept *affirmations of leadership.* When members take the time to let the leadership of the church know that the members value leaders' contributions to the worship, care, and programmatic dimensions of church life, receive it as a gift.

The Point of Departure

When renewal began to take place in the church that I most recently served, the "old guard" had hit bottom. They faithfully stayed in their historical downtown location while most members had left, disgruntled by the decline of membership. A conversion of sorts took place for that remnant who birthed themselves in the firm conviction that something was wrong. Whether they liked it or not, things needed to change.

This congregation was able to make tough decisions, even though the decisions were uncomfortable and inconvenient. Acknowledgment of their desperation helped them to understand the urgency of the issues they were facing, and as a result, they were able to deal with the issues head on. It may be that, long before we look for better strategies or even more effective programs, we need to pray for more reality, more conviction about how much needs to happen both in our own lives and in the lives of congregations. Maybe we need to be shaken from our complacency and rediscover the adventure of faith that claimed our lives when we first came to know Jesus, when we had a faith that gave no room for nominal beliefs and passively held sameness. In the days of our first love with Jesus, we wanted to be the church and would have done anything to make it possible.

A REST STOP ALONG THE WAY

- Describe your congregation's atmosphere of encouragement, permission, and experimentation. Are you satisfied with it? Why or why not?
- What is your congregation's context? Consider community rhythms, social and economic demographics, and newer trends.
- Are there some destructive constructs currently at work in your congregation? If so, can you name them and begin to develop a plan to address them?

6

Missioning the Church

Travelers Packing for the Borderlands

BORDERLAND COMPASS POINT

There is intention involved in borderland living. It is like the difference between being a passive tourist or an active traveler. Travelers, the borderland dwellers, enter into living with the intent to experience, engage, embed, and embody the God who is already at work in our world. And travelers do not forget to pack the attitudes necessary for their adventure.

Our friends were "missioned" at their church the other day. It is a phrase that is strange to both the church tradition in which they had grown up and the one in which I serve. However, I was moved by the idea of "missioning" in part because it gives a word to the epiphany-like experience I had with my former congregation as described in the last chapter.

These friends are teachers–one an effective public school literacy expert and the other a widely recognized university professor of English and cultural studies. They are people of profound faith, passionate about their call to teach. The liturgical activities of the church they now attend are somewhat new to them, so they were surprised when the minister in charge of the congregation expressed concern that they had not been "missioned" for their upcoming school year.

Every year, members of this historic urban congregation go through an act of "missioning." People are brought forward in the worship service and confirmed in their "call" to work intentionally and incarnationally in ministry wherever they are. They are brought forward in the liturgy and, with words of commissioning, the sign of the cross is made on their hands and on their foreheads, signifying word and deed. Mothers working in the home are missioned. Lawyers are missioned. Everyone who desires to see their particular occupation or circumstance as a God-given place of ministry and call takes part in this moving and deeply intentional act of worship in the church.

"Sunday Christians" are irrelevant in today's world. William Diehl, in his book *The Monday Connection*, points out, "What does it profit a person to worship God for one hour in a church on Sunday but be unable to experience God's presence in the Monday world?"[1] Even more, what does Sunday morning piety mean if the result is not a challenge to live a more missionary life in the places we spend our lives?

Why Do We Not Mission People?

Maybe we do not "mission" people into their workplaces because we ultimately need them to serve the structures inside the church. Too often outside activities are perceived as sideline activities of little value except for bringing people into the circle of programmatic ministry. The inside programs of the church, such as Sunday school, youth ministry, women's groups, Bible study, fellowship, and worship, are perceived to be the real activities of the church. As a result, there is little time left over for the so-called extracurricular activities of ministry out in the community.

This mind-set is often confirmed when I consult with declining churches. When asked for reasons they want the church to grow, they produce a myriad of concerns focused on their fear of dying. New people represent survival and resources to continue what they are already doing. While well intentioned, these reasons are inadequate. Their bumper stickers would read, "We don't want to die," and their assumptive motivation is gathering people to continue what has always been.

A foundational theology is at work in this situation, one with which I do not agree. The great motivator in this attitudinal frame for church life has been the disastrous notion for some that the proper home for Christians is heaven and, if not there, then the church must do. We are just passing through and, consequently, merely hanging on until something better comes along. The emphasis is on spiritual evacuation to a better place, and church life is simply a waiting room of activity. The sacred and secular are separated as a direct result of such a theological position. The impact is the perpetuation of a dichotomy that bestows different values on the places in which faith is lived. The Christian holding this theological frame sees activities in the secular world as distraction from the higher activity of life in the sacred space of church.

Why We Should "Mission" People

This view of the church and its ministry is neither scripturally relevant nor programmatically helpful. In his life and teachings, Jesus introduced us to the idea that his reign, the kingdom of God, is not just a spiritual notion encouraging us to get people into heaven. It is a current reality. It is not quite attained, but it is a taste of what might be. We, as followers of Jesus, are called to live out those possibilities of godly reign incarnationally and communally. The call is to build a church community that is more engaged and active in the world as well as in the sacred task of community building within the church.

Christ came to announce and demonstrate the present and coming kingdom of God. Under God's reign in Christ the whole world was and is being redeemed. "The church's mission," Robert Webber therefore states, "is to be the presence of the kingdom."[2] Newbigin wrote, "In every culture Jesus is introduced as one who bursts upon the culture's models with the power of the wholly new fact that God reigns over the whole world through Jesus Christ."[3]

The church becomes both an instrument and sign of what God wants to do in this kingdom that Jesus brought to earth. The purpose of the church and its mission is to incarnationally point to what it might look like when a community of people becomes alive under God's reign. By "missioning," the church is making visible to each member, to the church community, and to the world that God's people are at work.

A few years ago, someone tragically ended the lives of five Amish girls while they were at school. The Amish people, rooted in peacemaking, had their world brutally interrupted with irrational violence by a person from a world that they were taught to shun. People throughout the nation responded to the tragedy by setting up a fund for the families who lost loved ones. The Amish did something very different. They set about loving, forgiving, and caring for the family of the killer. News reporters were shocked that these people were not reacting with cries for vengeance or retribution. They expressed a grudging admiration for their compassionate response and were confronted with a people who were demonstrating what William Willimon prophetically observes when he writes that "the gospel is not a set of interesting ideas about which we are supposed to make up our minds. The gospel is intrusive news that evokes a new set of practices, a complex of habits, a way of living in the world, discipleship."[4] The community of faith represents a new kind of living both together and into the world.

George Hunsberger clarifies that the New Testament never says we are to build or extend the reign of God. The kingdom is a gift and inheritance. In Luke 12:32, Jesus tells the disciples, "Do not be afraid, little flock; for it is your Father's good pleasure to give you the kingdom." Our role as the people of God is to "receive" and "enter" into its possibilities. Hunsberger continues:

> Daily life becomes a discipline of asking how one may move more squarely into the realm of God's reign and how one may welcome and receive it into the fabric of one's life this day more than ever before. Here as well one can find a more focused way of living together as the community of Christ... The community of the church would testify that they have heard the announcement that [there is a God who reigns in love and that his] reign is coming, and indeed is already breaking into the world.[5]

Capturing the "missioning" mind-set will impact the way we live out the rhythm of kingdom living. It is a key theme in the church's larger task as the body of Christ sent into the world to be a witness in word and deed. By living in the "missioning mind-set," the church moves into the borderlands of engagement where Christian faith, other faiths, and unfaith intersect. To choose to do anything less simply produces an inability to live authentically as the church.

A Traveler or a Tourist?

Borderland living as a missioned member of the kingdom is both a corporate decision and an individual choice. The church missioned our friends but they were still required to embrace the journey. Their decision boiled down to two options: Would they approach the journey as travelers, or as tourists? There is a difference between the two, one that is not difficult to see. My present work requires a lot of travel. As I prepare for each trip, I must decide on the itinerary, on my goals, even on the contents of my suitcase. These smaller decisions are determined by the larger choice that I make between approaching the trip as a traveler or tourist.

I frequently visit Kenya. I spend much of the time there in places where tourists do not go. On occasion, however, I will travel into Nairobi and have tea at the Norfolk Hotel. The Norfolk is a stately relic of the past situated in the downtown of the city. I love its terrace because it overlooks the parking area where people going on safari depart from and return to. It is quite a sight to watch these visitors alight from their safari vans and land cruisers, dressed in the khaki safari wear they purchased at the local mall back in North America before they left for the trip.

These are the tourists. Their driving tours to the Masai Mara are designed to avoid the poverty-stricken areas of the city, such as the Mathere Valley and Kibera, where almost two and a half million people live in horrendous conditions. Tourists would be appalled. Most of them never see the Nairobi and Kenya I have come to know because they have been guided away from those sights. Unfortunately, they leave Kenya thinking they have seen the country. In truth, their experience was mediated. It was almost an illusion, a make-believe and controlled world shaped for them.

Tourism, at its best, is always comfortable and convenient. One friend tells me that when he goes into the Hilton in a foreign country, he expects the hotel to be just like home. He may be right, because many travelers have similar expectations. It is rumored that when Conrad Hilton opened his hotel in Istanbul, he made the comment, "Each of our hotels is a little bit of America." After moments in a strange territory, tourists can return to the atmosphere that makes them feel safe and secure in its familiarity. Obviously, the interior decorators add bits of local atmosphere–tourists, after all, want their money's worth.

Tourists can sign up for tours that have group rates, which allow the trip to be less costly. Tourists get what they pay for. For a reasonable investment, they get a minimal experience where their stereotypes are confirmed and perhaps even heightened. They taste the other world, but they never immerse themselves deeply enough to truly understand it.

What the tourists encounter in the end is themselves, because the best tourist experiences confirm expectations. It is not an adventure that challenges and surprises in its difference. It is a pseudo-adventure of affirmed assumptions and realized expectations.

The difference between a tourist and a traveler is the degree of discomfort, risk, and personal investment that the trip requires. The cost of being a traveler is different. The traveler risks health and comfort, thinking outside the lines of stereotypes and assumptions because of immersion in the rhythms of the visited places. The traveler gains an expanded world, an adventure of surprises, and a deeper appreciation for the people encountered.

Many people treat faith and discipleship as tourists on a spiritual tour. It is like a foreign country they have heard about and would like to be able to say they have visited. So, like any tourist hoping for a good experience, they choose the sights they want to see and even make some strange purchases to help create memories. They are, however, unlikely to get on the bus if they think the journey they are about to take will involve risk or inconvenience.

A tour might seem the best way to go in the missional journey of following Christ into the world. After all, it at least gives a taste of the "sentness" without risking traveler's indigestion and inconvenience. You can keep all your prejudices, assumptions, and rhythms without having to make drastic alterations to either the church or even your individual faith. Your security and safety are still rooted in the familiar, and there is little risk, but, unfortunately, minimal impact as well. This pseudo journey is proving extremely destructive in North America.

The Four "E"s of Traveling in the Borderlands

Entering into borderland living requires a church to become a traveler of a different kind, companioning with God as all the dimensions of life are transformed within what David Augsburger calls "a cluster of practices of dissident discipleship."[6]

This vibrant transformational *experience* of personal as well as corporate faith makes all the difference. The mission of the church emerges from a vibrant and dynamic faith experience. It reveals itself as both a deepening experience of the soul and a reoriented focus in living responsibly and faithfully out as "sent" people of God.

Responsible living is made possible in the proactive desire to *engage* the neighborhoods and relationships that are God's gift to the church and the individual believer. These are not simply short forays of activity. They are revealed most incarnationally as ongoing proactive and consistent involvement. Followers of Christ *embed* themselves into the relationships, systems, and organizations of the neighborhoods and networks God has set before them, seeking to be genuine and transparent in all they do. They do this under the realization that they are to *embody* an alternative community of "salt" and "light."

Borderland churches understand that while they may have the words of life to speak into the culture, they must first gain a hearing. This requires a humble sensitivity, reflected in the willingness to take the position of a listener involved relationally rather than simply as a self-interested programmer in their midst.

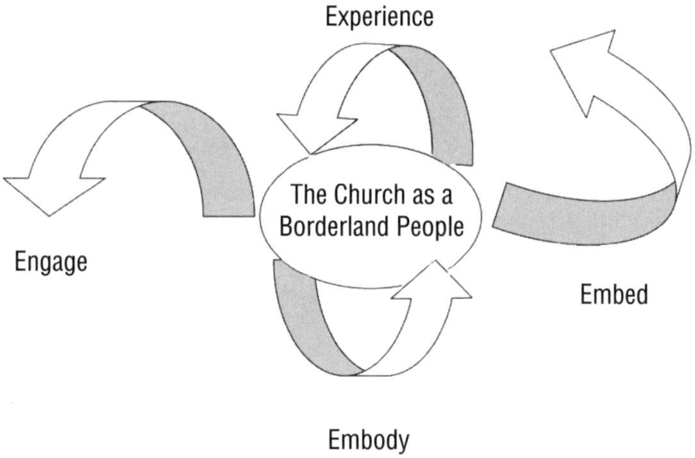

Experience: Being Shaped for Sentness

Faithful spirituality was always intended to be experienced long before it was talked about, but, somewhere along the way of Christendom living, we lost our moorings. We replaced this crucial aspect of faith with rationalistic approaches. In doing so, it became possible to discuss the faith, study it, and even live it outside of an encounter with God.

Paul expresses this truth in his second letter to the Corinthians. He points to the person who has encountered the comforting coming-alongside nature of God (2 Cor. 1:3–7). In the original Greek, this portion of scripture is a wordplay and, even in the English translation, you can sense its precision. He describes the idea of God's comfort (literally the coming-alongside nature of God) as first an experienced gift from God through which God "comforts us in all our troubles" (2 Cor. 1:4, NIV). But it does not end here. Paul affirms that out of personal experience comes an overflowing of "comfort' to others. He writes that God "comforts us in all our troubles so that we can comfort those in any trouble with the comfort we ourselves have received from God" (v. 4, NIV).

Christian spirituality is a holy longing for God that reveals itself not simply in cognitive understandings of God, nor even just in experiential encounters. It comes to its deepest fruition when it mirrors a passionate quest to see the things of God actualized in the world.[7] For example, our motivation for justice is not simply because of ideology. Because we have initially experienced justice from God, we can do nothing less for others. It transcends ideology because of our ongoing encounter with Christ. Ronald Rolheiser writes about it this way:

> For a Christian, the question of social justice has not only to do with truth, but also with energy, with motivation for the quest. Not just any motivation for justice is adequate since justice is not first of all a question of politics and economics, but a question of helping God build a kingdom of peace and for all.[8]

Discipleship is obedience emerging out of our encounter with God. It is a response to something that has happened to happen to us. Borderland spirituality shapes this experience further in the knowledge that God is already at work in the worlds around us. We are being flung out into the world only to join God in the work that is already taking place.

Augsburger develops this idea even further. He places this experience of God into three categories.[9] When we encounter the living God, a radical reorientation takes place because of this encounter with Jesus. In my words, we move from tourism to a risky life as a traveler. Traveling with Jesus requires a radical attachment not simply to a belief in Jesus but to a practical living out of the things that Jesus believed in. This results in a whole new way of living in our worlds, practicing responsible kingdom living. True spirituality will always contain at its core the living out of the presence of Jesus who makes obedience possible.

This raises an interesting dilemma for the church in North America. Lacking a faith that radically alters the way we live, we may find ourselves unable to grasp an understanding of what the good news is for others. We may still be able to articulate the bad news–"All have sinned and fallen short of the glory of God"–but that is all. Without an experienced faith, the ability to explain the good news for others disappears. We are unable to distinguish how it has been good news in our own lives.

Over the years as a pastor, I became aware that people found it difficult to articulate a clear understanding concerning how the gospel is good news to the people with whom they came into daily contact.

The leadership of our church began to set up focus groups to begin this journey of faith discovery. The groups were set up around professional or personal circumstances. Health professionals met together, as did teachers, stay at home moms, and so on. The pastoral staff facilitated discussions around five questions:

1. How would you describe your occupation, its joys and frustrations?

2. What are the greatest challenges you face in your profession? Life circumstance?
3. How does your faith intersect in your life and work?
4. What would the good news be for the people that you spend time with at work?
5. How can we as the church help you to be people of faith there?

The conversations were enlightening in both what was said and, frankly, in what was not. People did want to understand what their faith meant in these places, but had few words or even tools to do so. Beyond the "saying a little word for Jesus," many were unable to articulate an integrated and clear view of faith in the workplace. It was sad to watch the desperate looks that appeared on the faces of some longtime followers of Christ as they struggled with not only the faithful word to others but even the faithful impact on their own lives.

These dialogues did bring some great synergy. Out of these conversations emerged a new way of seeing the role of the church in the lives of the people who called this church their home. The leadership discussed how the church might better empower and walk alongside people who vocationally should be called to live out their faith in the marketplace of neighborhoods, occupations, and relationships. It altered the way we approached programming and even the content within those programs. By hearing what the struggles were, we found ourselves asking what needs to be experienced in faith first so that lived faith becomes relevant.

Engage: Getting to Know Your Borderlands

We are not passive cultural participants and neither are we objective cultural anthropologists encountering the "other" with the passive eye of an observer. Scrutinizing people from a position of aloof detachment may allow us to make superficial generalizations about people outside of the church. However, our faith is an involved faith that, from its outset, calls us to *engage* the world in very different ways.

My wife Carla has been a public school teacher for a number of years and, at one point of her career, she served as a guidance counselor in a large high school. Although I spent time with her there attending sports activities and social events with other teachers, I must confess my ignorance concerning the context in which she worked. I had my own personal experience at a high school, but that was all. One particular day, I came to the school at the exact moment the bell to dismiss classes rang. There I was in the middle of the hallway as adolescents poured out of classrooms, surrounding me in a stampede of noise, chaos, and conversation. I was taken completely by surprise. A look of horror came over my face in the realization this world was neither familiar or comfortable, but this was Carla's world for five days a week. It is doubtful that she understood my thoughts at that moment, but seeing my fear, she walked up and whispered in my ear, "Welcome to my world."

Our willingness and openness to explore these worlds is critical. If "church growth" in the last decades of the twentieth century was shaped by the idea of finding a location to place the buildings of the church that would maximize the possibilities for "come to" people to journey to us, borderland living as the church is about context of a different kind. The profound difference is a directional orientation, living into the context as opposed to inviting the context dwellers to come to us. This makes neighborhoods, workplaces, community sports leagues, and so many other places no longer optional for living out of faith. It makes them essential.

Embed: Living in the Borderlands

The broadest challenge facing most churches today in North America is not their willingness to engage the cultures around them or even the desire to understand them less superficially. The most profound challenge is the reconstruction necessary for church members to be freed up to live into their borderlands. These borderlands are places that have cultural, relational, and personal boundaries. They are complex systems of relationships and organizations that work together in some semblance of order and functionality. The tragedy is that when churches function apart from these realities, they develop rhythms and schedules that are often dissonant and counter to the boundaries and functionalities of the borderlands they wish to reach.

To truly engage our neighbors, we must "see" them, recognize their difference, honor their uniqueness, and respect the intrinsic values they keep whether or not we agree with them. The eyes that "see" emerge from the conscious willingness to *embed* ourselves in the network of relationships set before us.

Embedding is a place of mutual sharing that provides the possibilities of progressing into a deeper living commitment of understanding. This can be quite unsettling for a variety of reasons. We may be changed by the encounters. We may learn things about ourselves and about the other that causes us to transform our beliefs and practices. As they enter our churches, they may make us messier than we might have desired to be. A friend of mine once mused that the difference between a tourist and traveler (he used the word *pilgrim*) is that a tourist travels through a place but a traveler lets the place travel through him or her.

Missionaries go through a journey of discovery as they cross over into other cultures. The journey is never easy. They enter a significant process that over time transforms their lives. At first, all they see is the superficial behaviors and practices that are evaluated through the grid and filter developed from their past. As years pass, they live more intentionally and transparently into peoples' lives and it is then they discover more profound truths concerning the other. These discoveries invariably challenge their own premises and presuppositions and it is not uncommon for missionaries at that moment to begin a self-evaluation and inventory about what needs to change in their own lives. The truest, most authentic, relational engagements touch us deeply enough to warrant change on our part.

These relationships built on trust gradually move to places of deeper authenticity. People and cultures are complex, and the peeling back of the layers of understanding will take time and reciprocal transparency. Knowing, really knowing, someone or even a neighborhood is always to be framed in the context of the quality of relationship and earned trust.

A large church in an older suburban neighborhood functioned for years as a regional church oblivious to the community and neighborhood around it. In a burst of guilt, they decided to deliver plants to the homes around the church as an act of gratitude to neighbors who had put up with parking problems.

To their surprise, almost all of the plants were returned to the footsteps of their church. One of those plants contained a note of explanation. It read, "How dare you! You have shown little interest in our neighborhood. You have shown no concern for the needs of this community. We cannot accept your gift because you have always been an intrusion to us as neighbors. We will not be bought with this plant."

This rejection shook the church to its core. To their credit, they looked at themselves. They realized that they had simply used the neighborhood as a parking lot over the years, never perceiving themselves to be a part of it. Their parking lot had a chain link fence. The basketball hoops planted into the asphalt beside the church could only be used when the gate was open. They did not know their legislative representative in either the state or the city and they had no idea what the pressing needs were in the community. They were users and not participants.

Their reflections went further. They realized that the members, most of whom drove from other places in the city, used their own neighborhoods in much the same way. While the neighborhood around the church was like a parking lot, the neighborhoods of members were stopping off points with the majority of time and personal investment placed in the church and its programs.

For most congregants, nurturing the relationships and systems of their neighborhood were always secondary to the commitments required at the church. They began to understand that two very distinct issues required their attention. Engagement would require joining the clubs or the sports league where borderland people spend their energy. Maybe it would be spending time outside the office with the people with whom one works. Maybe it would be stopping to visit with a neighbor over the backyard fence. Whatever it took, it would require a willingness to reevaluate their priorities.

Embody: Living as an Alternative Community

Rocky had been attending worship for a number of months. His life was a story of years of alcohol and drug abuse. His warmth covered up the years of deterioration that his body had suffered due to that abuse. Every Sunday, he would shake hands with me at the door and say, "Vaya con Dios, Gary–that means, go with God." On many Sundays we would pause in the service to pass the peace of Christ. People would move through the sanctuary of the church and repeat words of peace giving to each other. "The peace of Christ be with you," one person would say to the other, who then would reply, "and also with you." Rocky grabbed my hand with great enthusiasm one Sunday as this passing of the peace was taking place. With passion he blessed me with words of encouragement, "pieces of Christ, Gary, pieces of Christ." I have come to realize that Rocky may have been right. The church is called to be "pieces of Christ" to the world.

The idea of pieces of Christ is a dominant theological image found in the New Testament idea of the body of Christ. Christ is most fully known when the community lives out being the body of Christ. This is a sacred task. We are asked to surrender our personal vision of God, the different tasks and unique gifts we bring to the table, and place them all into the context of a community of people seeking to *embody* what it means to be a kingdom people. We need each other if we are to be the fullest image of God in Christ. In the church (Rom. 12; Eph. 4; 1 Cor. 12) we surrender to a vision of God greater than our own so that we can be conformed into the image of Christ. We become the face of Jesus to the world, his hands and feet. There really is no way to make this any simpler. The difficulty is living it out.

If you have ever sat through a ceremony at which people become citizens of your country, you will understand this. At one point in our ceremony in Canada, the presiding judge talks to the new citizens about what it means to be a Canadian, of the way we approach life and each other and the values we hold. What I loved about that ceremony that day was how it caught me up in its wave of patriotism and made me want to live up to those standards. The judge defined who we are and who we are not, and I did not want to disappoint those responsibilities of citizenship.

That is what 1 Peter 2:9–10 tells the exiles to whom Peter is writing, that they are "a royal priesthood, a holy nation, God's own people." He is calling us to a particular set of core values that shape the way we live in society, neighborhoods, and communities.

In the letter of Diognetus in the early second century C.E., this pagan writer described these values this way:

> Christians do not live in cities of their own; they do not use a peculiar form of speech; they do not follow an eccentric manner of life... [A]lthough they live in Greek and barbarian cities alike, as each man's lot has been cast, and follow the customs of the country in clothing and food and other matters of daily living, at the same time they give proof of the remarkable and admittedly extraordinary constitution of their own commonwealth... They busy themselves on earth, but their citizenship is in heaven. They obey established laws but in their own lives they go far beyond what the laws require. They love all men, and by all men are persecuted. They are unknown and still they are condemned; they are put to death and yet they are brought to life. They are poor, and yet they make many rich; they are completely destitute, and yet they enjoy complete abundance.[10]

The impact of the church in the first century was directly related to the way Christians lived together, a lifestyle that gave outsiders a taste of a way of a better life, shaped by Creator God.

Neighbors, Natural Networks, and Neighborhoods

Whenever you enter a discussion on moving into neighborhoods, the conversation invariably transitions to the need to define what we mean by "neighbor." People make the observation that North American life is no longer simply a matter of geographically located relationships or even the nuclear family. Mobility has changed everything.

Mobility has become a dominant feature affecting our ability to develop deep, intimate, and lasting relationships. Stability of relationships has changed as well because of the varied lifestyle choices and the mobility factors in which people find themselves sometimes work against the desire for deep relationships.

The workplace has become a place where you spend an inordinate amount of time and, as a result, it plays a much deeper relational signifi-0cance than before. For a time, neighborhoods lost their significance in relationship building. Tragically, they have become places to stop at night and refuel before you head out again in the morning.

A friend of ours described her existence in a suburban community on the outskirts of a large metropolitan area. She observed that the garage doors would open in the morning as people left for work and do the same to receive the car on its arrival back into the home. These garage doors–opening and swallowing the cars only to spit them out the next morning–became a symbol of her isolation as she lived as the only stay-at-home mom on her cul-de-sac. Her experience of the loneliness of her existence was heightened each winter when neighborhood dwellers stopped venturing out into their yard because of the cold, only reappearing as the spring thaw brought them out again.

We also realize that some relationships are significant and others are not. Sociologists discuss the difference between the intimate and personal closeness of primary relationships and the casual and more superficial distance of secondary relationships. They mention, for instance, that most people have a capacity for only so many primary relationships in their lives. The primary relationships are usually the ones that you focus on the most. They emerge from the natural places you spend your time or focus your relational energies. So who is your neighbor?

The expert in the law in Luke's gospel story in 10:25–37 asked this exact same question, although he did so for different reasons than you and I might ask. He wanted to know what the "the minimal standard" was for neighbor love. After his attempt to trick Jesus into a theologically incorrect answer by asking him a question concerning the inheritance of eternal life, Jesus actually turns the table and traps the legal expert into a conversation that he did not want.

Jesus asks him what the greatest law of all was, and the man states quite emphatically: love the Lord your God with all your heart, and with all your soul, and with all your strength, and with all your mind; and love your neighbor as yourself" (10:27). The plot thickens when he asks the minimal question of superficial religious life, "And who is my neighbor?" (10:29).

This is the question that we ask when we really want to be told who we can ignore and who we must take seriously. It is a similar question to the one asked by Peter concerning forgiveness (Mt. 18:21–22). He wanted to know how many times he had to forgive someone. What we are really asking is how far we have to go to be a disciple. They help us sort how little has to be done to follow Jesus and have little to do with intimate and passionate discipleship. They serve to allow us to work out our discipleship at the minimal standard of disciplines and values while still feeling justified.

Jesus' reply to the "minimal standard" question of the expert of the law is to tell the parable that we have come to know as that of the good Samaritan. In this marvelous story we are told not only that the legal expert was asking the wrong question, but in fact that all listeners may be surprised who their neighbors may be. Our neighbors are not always the people next door, nor are they necessarily a part of our tribe or family.

The Greek word translated as "neighbor" in the New Testament focuses on the idea of location and relationship. It literally means "one who is nearby," but that does not necessarily mean geography. In fact, geography may have less to do with "being nearby" than frequency of time spent in the same environment. Your neighbors could be people with whom you meet regularly as coworkers. They may live in your neighborhood, not necessarily nextdoor, but, because of your involvement together in children's sports, you interact at numerous times around very focused activities. Socially, they are within your circle or network of relationships. Geography may have little to do with being a neighbor. It may have more to do with networks and interactions.

Your neighbors are not necessarily part of your family, but may sometimes be even closer than a family member in terms of intimacy. We are called to treat our neighbors in very particular ways. They may not be related but they are definitely part of our lives. We are told to "love your neighbor as yourself" (Mt. 19:19), and it is worth thinking about what this means in the light of borderland living. The litmus test for authentic neighbor love may be focused on the willingness to take the neighbor seriously.

Many followers of Christ who wish to move their lives into the borderland of missional living struggle at this point. They are unable to see the other because they have not rested in God's love for them. It is fascinating how many passages in scripture point to the fact that out of our relationship in Christ emerges an ability to live genuinely both in community and in the lives of what many might see as strangers and outcasts.

The core problem we face for effective borderland living is found in what one writer called the spine of identity. He says, "When the spine of identity is well established it is possible to risk relating in depth to those different then ourselves. When the spine of identity is weak, then everything is a threat."[11] If these words are true, then it becomes imperative to engage people from the place of grounded and faithful encounter with God. Without that rootedness, followers of Jesus remain intimidated and fearful of the worlds around them.

Effective borderland living will recognize the differences of others, focusing on the engagement in such a way as to embrace the neighbor with serious intent and honor while acknowledging the primacy of the "natural networks" of relationships as the fertile ground for interaction, community, and belonging.

What Are You Going to Pack for the Journey?

Traveling into these new worlds of borderland adventure will require certain necessities. Critical to the journey are specific attitudes as well as key items.

Imagination

Imaginative spirit is important in borderland living. David Bosch wrote, "...in light of a fundamentally new situation and precisely so as to remain faithful to the true nature of mission–mission must be understood and undertaken in an imaginatively new manner today."[12] Imagination allows the borderland to be a place of adventure and transformation. It flows from the ability of people living in the borderland to hope and to place their fears aside.

Fear can be understood as a lack of imagination. Our North American culture has created a false sense of security. Our fear of losing its safety has robbed us of our imagination and the courage to live boldly. Imagination is the wide-eyed wonder that people and circumstances can change, that things do not have to remain the same. Bosch once again speaks to this as he unpacks the missional imagination necessary for borderland living. It is an imaginative hope that sees the possibilities and wants nothing more than to see these possibilities take place. He writes:

> [T]he belief that things can be different...is creating almost boundless hope in the hearts of millions, particularly among the less privileged. The notions of repentance and conversion,

> of vision, of responsibility, of revision of earlier realities and positions, long submerged by the suffocating logic of rigid cause and effect thinking, have surfaced again and are inspiring people who have long lost all hope...at the same time giving a new relevance to the Christian mission.[13]

A Willingness to Be Surprised

Luke pictures the disciples at the beginning of the Acts of the Apostles, on the Day of Pentecost, as confused and squabbling, insular and afraid. Their petty jealousies and ambitions made them juggle for place in the loosely organized group. Luke tells us in Acts 2 that they gathered in the upper room, waiting. That says it all. Churches that lose their sense of anticipation, that no longer live open to the surprise of God, simply dry up waiting. They become predictable and stale. When this happens, they lack the ability to anticipate God at work and to recognize God's actions when they happen. Church life was not meant to be predictable. And, neither was it to be a comfort zone in which God is controlled. No wonder Annie Dillard says that we are too predictable in church. She suggests that we wear crash helmets to church because being a part of church should transform our lives and make us revolutionary followers of Jesus Christ.[14]

I experienced this in a worship service just after my graduation from seminary. I was preaching on Pentecost Sunday with the great anticipatory feelings that only newly graduated seminarians can have. My best work on this sermon focusing on the work of the Holy Spirit was to be shared with this "needy" congregation and I was sure that they needed all of my knowledge. In retrospect, it was a typical Pentecost sermon. The faithful had all heard these words from Acts 2 before, and very few preachers had given new insights to its content. I was neither able nor ready to give anything fresh, but God was. I began the description of how the church was birthed by the Holy Spirit, how tongues of fire descended and a great rushing wind entered the room.

At mention of that rushing wind, something marvelous took place. With a loud bang, a window in the sanctuary shattered and the sermon was interrupted with a breath-stopping object lesson. I will always remember the faces of the people on that day. For just a moment, with eyes wide, they sat in anticipatory awe.

I realize that it is not easy to live with anticipation all of the time. However, if faith is to have any meaning and significance, our worlds must be interrupted and our self-referential focus taken captive by a God who calls us to the willingness to be surprised.

Openness to Celebrate What Really Matters

I am intrigued by Jeremiah 9:23–24. It was written at a time when the people of God in Israel had lost touch with the commitments of justice, steadfast love, and righteousness that had been set down as foundational bases for their life together. They substituted for them with an admiration for wealth, power, and intellectual knowledge.

Jeremiah's words at the first part of this second chapter are words of weeping and wailing, and even a promise of destruction. Then, this cranky prophet sets the plumb line for what really matters and what really should be celebrated. It is a statement about what counts and what does not, about assumptions that we hold, about what is important and about how wrong we can be. The dilemma of the people referenced to in Jeremiah reminds me of an old joke I once heard about a psychologist who came to his patient and said, "I have good news and bad news. The good news is that you have a healthy self-image. The bad news is that it is not based on reality."

The people of God were dying from the inside out. Corruption and complacency were the order of the day. Intellectual wisdom, physical power, and wealth were the fundamental characteristics to be admired and everyone had bought into that value system. North American culture is built on these three values.

But listen to Jeremiah's counterpoint–his "Do you really want to know what matters?" statement. Self-sufficiency is juxtaposed to trusting in God. What really matters, we are told, is to have the good sense to know God as Lord and how God acts.

If we adopt disciplines of the faith so that we are formed more and more into the image of God, then the values closest to God's heart should become ours as well. Jeremiah describes what is nearest to the heart of God in terms of boasting. If you want to boast, he says, then boast in a God who you know "exercises kindness, justice and righteousness" (Jer. 9:24, NIV).

As discussed in previous chapters, the call to discipleship and being a taste of the kingdom of God in this world will require a radical approach.. This call cannot be avoided and it cannot be discovered without study, prayer, and transformational living. We cannot transform neighborhoods if we are not willing to be transformed by the things that matter to God.

Being Pragmatic

Engaging the communities around us really does need to move beyond the conversations about how nice it would be if we did it. It needs to transition from airy conversation to practical "Does it work?"

strategies. As ideas surface for engagement, the following questions are part of what you pack for the journey.

- Will this strategy make a difference?
- Will it build ports of entry into the community?
- Will it be the right port of entry? (That is, does it actually reach into the community and network of relationships in such a way that genuine and authentic relationships are built?)
- Will it put a face to the church and break down walls of misunderstanding?
- Will it enable us to participate in the transformation of the community or the workplace?
- Will it set people free? Give hope? Bring peace? Build faith and trust?
- Will it result in an emergence and deepening of Christian community in the church itself?
- Will it lead the people of the church out into the world?

Pack with the Possibility that You Will Never Return

I think back to Joshua's call to cross over the Jordan. He tells the people of Israel that they have not been this way before and that they will not be able to return. It would be dishonest on my part if I did not tell you that a decision to journey into the borderlands means that you will not be able to return to the way it was.

A few years ago, I was taken to the gravesites of the pioneer missionaries from our denominational mission organization, faithful ones who had traveled to India over two hundred years ago. The people leading the tour talked about the spirit of adventure and the commitment that was required by many of these great giants of the faith who left home and country to come to a strange land all because of God's call on their lives. Then I was told something I had never heard before. Most of these pioneers came with their bags packed in coffins rather than in trunks, understanding that many of them would not return.

We can do no less. The prime challenge to churches is to pack with the realization that they are fundamentally leaving their comfort and convenient zones of security. They will not be able to return to the way it was, even if they wanted to. So pack as if you are not returning.

Living in the Borderlands

Many examples of Christian communities "experiencing, engaging, embedding and embodying" gospel values come to mind.

However, one in particular stands out for me. It is the story of a group of Christian farmers in a small but thriving rural area on the prairie. In the 1970s, these farmers were confronted with the images of famine that appeared on their TV screens. Their experience of the gospel in their own lives drove them to frame a way to respond and, as a result, they have for years prophetically grown grain for distribution around the world through two organizations, the Canadian Food Grains Bank (CFGB) and The Sharing Way (TSW).

They grow these project crops alongside their own crops and then join together as a community of farmers for the harvest. One year, the snows threatened earlier than usual in Alberta and the pressure to bring in the grain before the first snow was even more immediate. Growing up on the prairies, I have a memory of driving on the highway late at night and seeing the lights of the combines still working in the fields in order to get the grain in before that first snow fall.

This remarkable group of farmers, joined by friends from the community, chose to harvest the grain from the plots reserved for the CFGB/TSW first in an incredible witness to the possibilities of thinking differently about our neighborhoods and our world.

These were the first fruits that they felt must be harvested before their own fields. They took a loss that year because of their decision to live out with profound witness the rhythms of God's reign. A colleague standing with those farmers a few months later overheard one farmer remark that it cost him $20,000 to not bring in his own crop that night. He said it was a significant loss for him that year but it was worth it to see grain loaded and shipped overseas to people in need.

A REST STOP ALONG THE WAY

- What difference would it make to your life of faith if you were "missioned"?
- Has your life in Christ been more like a tourist or a traveler in God's kingdom? Why?
- What is the "good news" for those with whom you spend most of your time?
- Who is your neighbor?

7

Mapping the Journey

Moving into the Borderlands

BORDERLAND COMPASS POINT

The call to live as the church in the borderlands is a way to help the church of the twenty-first century recapture its essential missional nature. This final chapter offers five examples of borderland cases and identifies key indicators of their effectiveness. The chapter ends with a reflection on Jeremiah 29:4–9, verses that are God's answer to the cry of the exiles in Psalm 137.

The aim of presenting the missional nature of the church using the metaphor of the church in the borderlands has been to offer another way to emphasize the radical nature of the Christian faith. In the first century, the focus was as on the creation of a new community, a new way of relating together in our humanity, which resulted in a people that "were one in heart and mind...and shared everything they had" (Acts 4:32, NIV). In no time has it been more important to take the formation of that community seriously.

Rodney Clapp prophetically calls for churches to know who they are. He writes:

> I am arguing that the church should be distinctive, that it should live by its own self-understanding as a community constituted and sustained by the lordship of Christ. And according to that very self-definition, the church does not exist for itself, but for its mission and witness to the world on behalf of the kingdom.[1]

The borderland church understands that it is primarily a missional community of people being trained and equipped to live among the world as missionaries. Borderland Christians see their primary role as missionaries. The principles that missionaries applied in their pioneering efforts in previous centuries in the global South are now the principles for our world. God calls us to immerse ourselves in the culture. I love the way that Eugene Peterson captures this in his translation of John 1:14 in the Message, "The Word became flesh and blood and moved into the neighborhood." We can do no less.

In many ways the call to live as the church in the borderlands is a return to our biblical roots. This will require a radical shift in how we do church today. For most of our churches, the challenge is right here. My assumption throughout this book has been that the Christian faith and the church either lives a missionary existence or it is not the church. The missionary dimension of the church derives its energy from the nature of God, who, by nature, is a sending God.

I have often been asked if I see any hope for today's North American church. My response is always an unabashedly positive "yes." I believe in her possibilities and missional task. My greatest frustration is how ineffective the church has been in engaging our culture. I wish it was simply a matter of just doing more evangelism, worshiping in more contemporary ways, or being more committed to the things we hold dear. We have become passive in our approaches to ministry while a whole world of people live and breathe outside our current sphere of influence. Deep shifts are required in the churches' attitudes and relationships. It is time to reshape ourselves in such a way that the church of Jesus Christ becomes a movement, creating a new community and a new way of relating together that results in a people who are one in heart and mind...and shared everything they had (Acts 4:32, NIV). I am convinced that this is the hopeful future of the church.

It is exciting for me to see many churches making this shift back to the roots of missionary engagement. My purpose in this last chapter is to look at some borderland examples–churches small and large, rural and urban that are making the shift with transformational results.

Borderland Case #1: The Nations Next Door

A small church located in an established residential area of a city in the heart of the prairies is home to a few members whose missional direction has helped shift the church's identity and is having an international influence. Over the last few years, foreign students, mostly from Mainland China, have come to this city to attend the nearby university for post-graduate studies. They arrive with an eagerness to understand North American culture, including its faith systems, and a desperate need to be welcomed.

Several members of this local church volunteer with the on-campus Christian ministry group that works with international students. They attend all the events (many of which conflict with in-house church activities), bring buckets of food, and patiently chat with students whose English-speaking ability is very low.

The students' needs surface naturally. They want more intentional practice time with the English language. They need instruction on car maintenance and housing rentals. They need assistance with the preparation of unfamiliar foods and child-care help. All of these areas are addressed in Saturday afternoon English classes, special seminars, and on-going shared meals in the homes of these church members who are now honorary parents and grandparents to literally dozens of leading academic researchers worldwide.

Over the years, this ministry has provided many opportunities for the investigation of the Christian faith. Once, nine university professors from Mainland China landed at this university for a semester's exchange. Three of the professors appeared at the English as a Second Language class run by the church on Saturday afternoons staffed by the church members. During a break, one of the professors invited one of the church members to lead a study on Basic Christianity. These professors began to explore the possibilities of life in Christ and today continue their relationship with Christ back at their home universities in China.

These church members neither consider themselves gifted in evangelism nor as having aggressive personalities. Rather, their gentle and kind ways seem to be open to the possibility of sharing their lives, including their homes, their bicycles, their dishes, their time, their lawn mowers and snow-shovels, and their church. Service to others and welcoming hospitality are the foundations of a missional attitude to a world that has come to their neighborhood.

These members have lives that were radically changed by Jesus Christ. Most of them became Christians years ago and nurtured a vibrant relationship that they know makes a difference in their day-to-day living. There is no secret to effective communication of the gospel in word and deed. Neither is it as complicated as we are prone to make it. Effective communicators of the gospel have a story to tell of a God whom they encountered in the person of Jesus Christ, and this encounter causes them to live in different ways. Effective churches and followers of Jesus Christ live joyfully and fully into the worlds that God has placed before them.

Our world needs active involvement from committed followers who refuse to look the other way. The borderland followers want to impact and, perhaps just as important, be impacted by the world around them. They are willing to be changed by the encounter. If we want our hearts to look more like the heart of Jesus, that likeness will only come through participation in the borderlands. No authentic mission takes place from safe distances. Mission with integrity will not be found in convenient and comfortable conditions.

By embracing our neighbors in the borderlands, we portray a willingness to be involved. We engage in the real kingdom activity and, as a result, experience our true salvation.

Key Indicators from This Borderland Example:

- Members nurtured a vibrant and dynamic faith over the years and built their ministry on this foundation.
- The church decided on their own "bite-sized chunk" of God's mission to the borderland of their world in their particular city.
- The members understood that they could not do everything but, at the same time, realized that there was something they could do.
- Members shaped the ministry they developed to the reality of their congregational makeup.
- They built their ministry on real possibilities dictated by their context and the realistic limitations of their congregation.
- They kept it simple and built on their strengths.
- They kept their strategies simple and relational.
- They built this borderland strategy on hospitality and service.
- They understood that their commitment would require time and inconvenience.
- They committed themselves for the long haul, opening up their homes and even their church building at times often inconvenient to the church community.

Borderland Case #2: Captive to the Desire of Becoming More Like Jesus

Borderland churches believe that becoming what some call "a fully devoted follower of Jesus Christ" is for everyone. They see themselves as journeying toward a deeper sense of discipleship. For them, the journey is more important than the position in which they find themselves at any particular moment. The most relevant criterion is whether or not one is moving closer to Jesus. This is all that matters. Progress and growth is marked by behaviors and values that witness to the way Jesus is transforming the people we encounter and us. Are we becoming more and more a reflection of God's reign?

This borderland church celebrates the people who take their neighborhoods seriously and get involved. People in the workplace who develop relationships of friendship with their work mates are affirmed. The public schoolteacher faithfully living out her vocation from Christ at the high school is the hero. The stay-at-home mom who volunteers at the local community center to teach computers to immigrants is encouraged. Everything is about empowering all people wherever they are. When they gather together, their worship is a shared celebration of God movements into the world.

The church portrays evidence of growing, changing, and even deepening its skills and habits of discipleship. Nurturing citizenship in the reign of God is an overall priority of the church for all members of the community of faith.

This borderland church, known for its multiple services and many programs, recently looked intently at its ministry. Realizing that its effectiveness had predominantly been measured by attendance on Sunday worship and participation in mid-week programs, this group of believers made the decision to intentionally develop a new set of indicators for effectiveness. The indicators are simple but radically different from what they had been: all programs and ministries would now be evaluated by community impact and global impact measurements developed by the leadership team. Everything they do now passes through these two filters.

Changing the measurements of success and effectiveness takes time, but the results can be transformational. New frameworks of ministry have emerged. Small groups, ministry programs, and worship have been reshaped around refreshing missional themes. Ways of managing growth and creating intimacy and care through the use of small groups were changed. Each small group is now part of the missional intent of the church and each carries a missional commitment. Discipleship has become the congregational emphasis by which programs are designed to equip and nurture people.

Key Indicators from This Borderland Example:

- The church sees discipleship for borderland living as a lifelong process.
- Prayer has become a central activity in discipleship formation.
- As new participants come into the community of faith, they can sense this emphasis and are encouraged and equipped to integrate their lives with the practices and habits of life in the reign of God.
- Members can point to ways in which they are being transformed both in spiritual disciplines and value-forming behaviors.
- The church provides multiple ways that people can be trained, nurtured, and encouraged in their borderland living.
  - ~ They allow for a variety of entry points so that people of different ages and experiences are not left out.
  - ~ They understand that people learn in different ways and disciple-making must have a repertoire of variety if all are to follow Jesus Christ more fully.
- Church members can identify kingdom values that cause them to differ significantly from the borderland culture in which they are living incarnationally.
  - ~ They reflect less of a church culture and more of a kingdom framework. The things Jesus believed supersede their comfort and convenience.
  - ~ They discuss values such as attitudes about money, justice, compassion, truthfulness, and servanthood.
  - ~ They live demonstrating generosity and hospitality to others.
- The stranger does not frighten them.
- The pastoral leaders understand servanthood and share leadership with others. They are not afraid of others leading.
- The church is organized in such ways so that all people can participate in an atmosphere that is open to change, willing to experiment and even to fail.
  - ~ Dialogue is constantly being framed as a "best practice" conversation that allows for growth and getting it right.

Borderland Case #3: Becoming Surprisingly Attractive

When this young pastor came to his new pastoral charge, he wondered how he and his family would fit into this small rural community in the Midwest. It was a farming community built around a lake. However, this community also had some of the best hunting ground in the area. He began his education of the community by hanging out regularly at the coffee shop in the town. This was the place where the rangers and law enforcement officers hung out, and, over a period of time, their conversations turned to the serious need for more firearms training sessions, a requirement to receive a hunting license.

This pastor, lost in agricultural conversations, had a background in firearm safety and this became his ticket into the life and rhythms of the place both for himself and his church. Realizing that everything in this area was built on relationships and that he was an outsider, the pastor offered his services as a teacher for the firearms safety class. To say that the rangers were a little disconcerted is an understatement. Their need, however, was great and so the rangers reluctantly agreed. The young pastor, with the consent of his church, began his journey into the borderlands of engagement in a context into which few pastors had gone before.

Teaching the class was an incredible gift. Over time, it provided a place where relationships could be built. His winsome humor gave a face not only to the pastor but to his church as well. People who normally would not darken the doors of the church, no matter how good the worship or how welcoming the church was, were given an opportunity to relate to people of faith on their terms and they all flourished in the encounter.

For the pastor, these classes provided an intentional way of building trust with both the students who took the course and the rangers who hosted the classes. Familiarity may sometimes breed contempt, as the saying goes, but it more likely breeds trust, and this is exactly what occurred.

Slowly the rangers realized that this young pastor and his family were actually very nice people. The classroom encounters had led to invitations to have some of the rangers over to their home for supper, and these times with their families interacting together broke down walls of distrust and prejudice. Friendships grew with church members as well, and the impact of the church in the community grew with them. The church was now more aware of the real issues in the community because the members had relationships and conversations outside of their subculture.

One day one of the rangers appeared at the door of the pastor's home. He arrived with the carcass of a deer that had been confiscated from a poacher earlier that day. The ranger was asking for the use of the church's freezer in order to preserve the meat, which he was offering to the pastor for anyone whom he might know had need. That is exactly what occurred. The deer turned into a source of food for a number of people on limited incomes and this one gift morphed into a continued source of meat from the rangers.

Eventually the church took this gift further by then realizing that the community needed a food bank in the community. In partnership with the rangers, town council, and police, the food bank was established.

Rangers met church members. Together they grew in appreciation for each other through relationships. When issues came up in the community, the church was no longer on the margins of these concerns. Now, it is at the center of the conversations and often invited in from the very beginning. Today, people respect the church for the incarnational presence it offers.

Key Indicators from This Borderland Example:

- The church and its leadership study scripture and begin to redefine themselves as "sent" people.
  - ~ They realize that the most important thing that they do as the church is to serve as representatives of the reign of God.
- They realized that they were in desperate need to reintroduce themselves to the community.
  - ~ The community needed faces that they could connect to the church.
- People can articulate examples of the church's positive involvement in their lives.
  - ~ They understand that who these church people are has something to do with their faith.
- Borderland churches are able to pray meaningfully.
  - ~ They are informed about their community so that when they pray as Jesus prayed, "Thy kingdom come," they are able to tell you what that might mean in their community.
  - ~ These prayers excite them and lead them into missional living.
  - ~ They take periodic prayer walks around the town, asking God to work.
- They recognize the "not yet" of their ministry and are open to new ways to fulfill their calling while at the same time demonstrating faithfulness to what they are already doing.

- The church tells the stories of their community ministry both in its individual and corporate expressions.
  - They celebrate them in a way that people are affirmed in their discipleship.

Borderland Case #4: Living in "Uniform"

It is difficult to imagine that even the Salvation Army could lose a sense of its roots, but, in some major cities, social work and justice programs have replaced the incarnational presence of a local church. Suburban congregations within the Salvation Army thrive, but many of the congregations located in inner-city and downtown areas often struggle.

This is not the case, however, in at least one large metropolitan area I know. In this location, this particular church has witnessed the resurgence of borderland church life in one of the most difficult regions of their city. A group of young Salvationists with generational roots desired to recapture the synergy and passion of their movement's past. They moved back into the city in an intentional and incarnational way and chose to take up residence there.

If borderland churches are God's representatives in the world, then God's heart should frame their goals. This fledgling congregation became a visible and tangible taste of the good news of Jesus Christ. It regularly speaks for the voiceless in the community, standing with them in difficult times. The church's worship service is as eclectic as the community, for it is an amazing fusion of old Salvation Army hymns and contemporary worship music complete with a reggae beat.

While some suburban churches fight about the brass bands and uniforms of their tradition, in this inner city community both are wonderful contributions to the ethos. They represent progress in terms of discipleship. It turns out that in this context, uniforms are actually a plus. Becoming a soldier and getting your uniform are an amazing celebration. The community recognizes the uniform of church people as a positive symbol. It represents a people whose word and deed are woven together in integrated action. Church members are not afraid to walk their talk, and the community at large respects them for it.

Perhaps the most dangerous aspect of the non-borderland understanding of doing church is treating church members as if they are volunteers rather than disciples. This framework treats church participants as customers to be assimilated into the institution's life. Treating church members as customers can result in the creation of a consumer mentality in the church that ultimately works against calling people to a discipleship frame as faithful followers to Christ. It can result in a discipleship that is comfortable and convenient. Randy Frazee writes about this problem:

> The church must be careful not to confuse an assimilation strategy for church involvement with a spiritual formation model for community building. Both are necessary, but they are very different. An assimilation strategy defines how one gets involved in the life and programs of a church; a spiritual formation model defines the essential outcomes the church is attempting to get working into the lives of the people of the church.[2]

If borderland churches are a visible demonstration of how the good news of Jesus Christ transforms people to reflect more faithfully God's intentions for creation, then they are known most often by the actions they take outside of their comfort zones. They call people to visible and effective participation in God's activity in the world. As a community, they are being formed into a people that proclaim the good news in word and deed. You only have to ask one question to know if these people are actually impacting their borderlands. Go around the community and ask, "When you think of that church, what do you think of?" The answers will tell you everything.

Key Indicators from This Borderland Example:

- They are passionate about proclaiming the good news in both word and deed.
  - ~ They understand that audible proclamation is not simply focused on salvation but also on transformation–individually, corporately, and systemically.
  - ~ They realize that these transformations are a sign of the reign of God.
  - ~ They understand that proclamation is also visible. How we live among borderland people authenticates the good news and its validity.
- They understand that how they live as a community of faith is crucial to their witness to the world.
  - ~ Therefore, the church practices love and sacrificial service that declare to people in the wider community that faithful living out of kingdom values of truthfulness, servanthood, and compassion is possible.
- The church stands in solidarity with the borderland people around community concerns.

  - ~ When they differ or disagree, they still are perceived to stand together.
  - ~ Church members can articulate times and places in which they have stood with the community.
- Borderland agencies and organizations know about the church and speak positively of it.
- Their worship reflects the local community.
- People describe the community life of the church as "real" and people feel free to be themselves.
  - ~ They are able to see a community of people who believe, struggle, doubt, sin, forgive, and praise.
- Numerical growth is simply one among many measures of success.
  - ~ They measure the journey to a quality of ministry, service, and life together.
  - ~ They annually review these measurements for quality control and further development.
- A growing proportion of the people who make up their church are former borderland people.

Borderland Case #5: Walking the Talk

Two of my colleagues work and live in Beirut, Lebanon. Their personal story is one of transformation and convergence. They did not know each other growing up in Lebanon, but during the conflicts and civil war of the 1980s, they each separately made the choice to immigrate to Canada. Both left their home country with a distinct and passionate desire never to return to Lebanon.

Through a series of events, they each renewed their faith in Jesus Christ and began to attend the same Arabic-speaking church in the Canadian city in which they were living. This is where they first met, fell in love, and got married. But the story does not end here.

Over the next several years, they prospered in their occupations and in their faith. Because of Elie's leadership at the church, he began taking classes at the local seminary in a program designed for laypeople who need to continue in their professions but want to study theology, particularly missional theology. He graduated with his master's degree and continued in his occupation as one of the leading information technology consultants in the city. Mirielle's decorating business thrived as well and together they bought their dream home.

Their church became a place of nurture and ministry, but something strange occurred: they both felt that God was calling them back to Lebanon. The voice came in light of a call for Elie to become the provost at the Baptist Seminary in Beirut, and both of them, challenged by the possibilities, made the decision to go.

Eight months after their arrival, bombs began to fall again in Lebanon. The relative calm of recent years was interrupted by hatred, animosity, and strife.

Back during the war of the 1980s, most evangelical Lebanese Christians had tried to stay out of the way. Something very different took place in the churches and leadership around Beirut during the conflict of the past few years. This time, the new missional approach that was being studied in seminary and a deeper sense of challenge about being the church in the world caused them to look at this war in different ways. When the bombs began to fall, church leaders and seminary personnel gathered in prayer and came out of those meetings believing that this was a God moment for them. It was time to move into the borderlands.

In a matter of hours, Christians mobilized and decisions were made to open the Baptist high school in Beirut to accept refugees. Shortly after that, the seminary followed suit and over seven hundred displaced adults and children were given shelter. Scriptures such as, "when I was hungry, you gave me food," came to life in the compassionate responses to the displaced victims of a senseless war. Christians giving solace and comfort to displaced Muslims became an incredible witness to the hopeful and transformational nature of the gospel of Jesus Christ. These borderland followers of Christ provided food, medical care, emergency housing, and a taste of God's reign in the midst of the bombs.

Over the weeks that these people lived together, walls were broken down and bridges of conversation, compassion, and care were built. Resources were stretched–even the water supply at the seminary was drained and another well had to be built. With a chuckle, Elie tells the story about this event because the water well drill looked strangely like a rocket launcher. A special prayer meeting was held to pray for clear eyesight for the fighter pilots who might make that mistaken observation. As acts of compassion and care were taking place, groups were consistently praying throughout the city in the knowledge that God's presence was deeply at work at the time.

By the end of the crisis, new friendships had been established that have provided opportunities for ministries of care and incarnation. Christians also experienced a refreshing taste of the Spirit of God as their faith came to life through action. Having moved into the borderlands and tasted of the adventure of faith, it becomes increasingly difficult to go back to the way it was.

Key Indicators from This Borderland Example:

- Borderland churches are consumed with a desire to discern God's specific missional call for their community of faith.
- Borderland churches give visible evidence that their life, work, witness, and worship are influenced and shaped by scripture.
  - ~ Members openly seek to believe and behave in ways that conform to the gospel of Jesus Christ.
- Church members believe that the church exists to be an expression of Christ's love.
- The first question they ask when presented with a new idea or strategy is, "Why not?"
- They welcome the stranger into their homes, their church, and their lives. This contributes to the transformation of life and society.
- Prayer is central to everything they do and they recognize that prayer is a key aspect of being accountable to one another.
  - ~ They pray for one another.
  - ~ They pray for those with whom they differ and whom they dislike.

Borderland Case Commonalities

Borderland church members are busy connecting with people and engaging the world. Their message is not passively framed in the hopeful desire that people may come to their programs. Neither is their worship designed to attract people whom they do not know.

The purpose of the church is to be found in God's missional intent. God calls the church to discern, celebrate, and participate in mission. This will require the formation of a community of disciples willing to be a sign, taste, and incarnational witness of the reign of God. The call of the church is to enter and engage in the places where God is already at work because they believe that God is moving long before they show up. The adventure of faith is discovering what God is already doing and joining in.

Becoming a borderland church will require the shaping of a radically new vision for most churches. It will necessitate new ways of thinking and new patterns of behavior. Church leaders may have to retool for skills, support, and resources that enable them to lead this adventure of borderland living and to shift toward a direction that looks something like the chart on the next page.

“Come to” Church	“Go to” Borderland Church Living
Passive “Field of Dreams” mentality: Build and plan good programs and they will come.	Proactive engagement with the culture and context: The church will come to the community.
Disconnected from the community around it: Members are users of the community rather than participants in it.	Defines itself by who they are outside the church building: Sees the community and networks of relationships as places of discipleship and service.
Observational and reactive	Interactive and intentional
SWAT team mentality	Incarnational and natural
Predictable and programmatic	Experiential and experimental
Propositional and positional	Participatory and process-oriented

God Replies to the Psalmist’s Questioning Cry

Captive in an unwanted world, void of familiar rhythms and themes, the psalmist cries out, “How can we sing the songs of the LORD while in a foreign land?” (Ps. 137:4, NIV). I believe that God’s response to that plaintive cry is captured poignantly in Jeremiah 29. From verse four to verse eleven, the prophet informs the exiles of God’s response to their plight. At first, God’s response may appear to lack compassion for the psalmist’s deep sense of alienation and dislocation. The words certainly do not assuage the angry vengeful feelings so sadly illustrated in the last few verses of Psalm 137. He is mad at the Babylonians for what they have done to him and his people, and only slightly less angry at God for allowing it to happen.

God’s reply may only heighten his frustration. It appears that it was God who sent them into exile in the first place. They have been wrenched out of Jerusalem and dragged to Babylon, and God makes it clear that he indeed is the cause. In fact, God mentions it twice:

> This is what the LORD Almighty, the God of Israel, says *to all those I carried into exile* from Jerusalem to Babylon: Build houses and settle down; plant gardens and eat what they produce. Marry and have sons and daughters; find wives for your sons and give your daughters in marriage, so that they too may have sons and daughters. Increase in number there; do not decrease. Also, seek the peace and prosperity of the city to which I have carried you into exile. Pray to

the Lord for it, because if it prospers, you too will prosper." (Jer. 29:4–9, NIV, italic added)

While these frustrating words may be difficult to hear, they state a critical truth for a people fearful of the future, angry at the present, or simply paralyzed to do anything about the reality of a broken world. The words are frustrating because the people did not ask to be part of this kind of world. They did not choose to live in those times. Nor have we today. So what do we do with the fact that God put us here?

If these times are a form of exile in comparison to the times in which we grew up, God intentionally put us here. To grasp this biblical truth is to realize that the people of God are always called to be a people for the time and place God has placed them. The challenge is to help churches understand that this time and this place are a God-given actuality. We do not live in that past. This is the time and place in which God has intentionally placed us.

God's answer to the exiles' dilemma comes with a pragmatic command, challenging them to live in their present. "Build houses and settle down; plant gardens and eat what they produce. Marry and have sons and daughters…Increase in number there; do not decrease" (Jer. 29:5–6, NIV). In other words, invest, participate, and even grow in this place. Do not just hang on. Believe things can change. Believe that you can make a difference where you are.

Calling them to plant gardens is God's way to challenge the people to settle in for a time. No one invests in planting a garden or building a home if they feel that their time is limited in a place. God's strange words are a challenge for the exiles to do something opposite and unnatural to what they would like to do. They wanted out. God wanted them to settle in and participate in this foreign world even in the grieving for the familiar and comfortable. When we want to get out, or just fearfully hang on, God's call by God to settle in may prove frustrating. But it is, however, how borderland followers of Christ live most fully.

Jeremiah's words are really God's way of saying, "Deal with it! This is the world in which I have placed you." Verse eleven is often pulled out and quoted out of context because it is a promise of presence. But the promise is conditional to living presently in their exile. "For I know the plans I have for you," declares the Lord, "plans to prosper you and not to harm you, plans to give you hope and a future" (Jer. 29:11, NIV). We will not be left alone in this borderland journey. God will be with us.

This is as true now as it was then. God is asking us to sing the new song, do new things, be creative in this world, and live as if we are going to be here for a long time. The prophetic words of verse 7 provide an interesting concept, "Seek the peace and prosperity of the city to which I have carried you into exile. Pray to the LORD for it, because if it prospers, you too will prosper" (NIV). The principle is simple: if you want a better Babylon then actively work for its well-being. From a borderland perspective, if we want to make a better neighborhood, city, or society, then we need to live in it intentionally and incarnationally. If we bring "shalom" to this place, it will be a better place for us as well.

Early in the 1900s, William Booth prepared a telegram to be sent out to all the Salvation Army personnel around the world. His desire was to write something that would inspire his movement, but the cost for sending a telegram was so high that he realized that he could only afford to send out one word. He carefully and prayerfully chose a word that would forever embody the mission of the Salvation Army. The word was "others." That one word captures the mission of the church and the reason for our existence as the people of God.

Jesus spoke similar words in his Sermon on the Mount. The mission of the kingdom that he announced and brought into being was to be salt and light in the city (Mt. 5:13–14; Lk. 13:21). We are useless if we lose these traits. In Jeremiah, God speaks similar words of command to the exiles when he says, "Seek the peace of the city."

The word translated as "peace" in English in this passage comes from the Hebrew word *shalom.* It literally means wholeness, soundness, a bringing together of all the pieces into one. To live in shalom is to be "saved" in the deepest sense of that word's meaning. In the context of a world out of step with God and out of step with itself, the good news of Jesus Christ is that shalom is possible.

The implications of seeking "shalom" are enormous. Seeking "shalom" serves as the core value of all ministry activity and direction for borderland churches. For example:

- *Shalom* creates community. The mission of the church is to establish a community of faith reconciled to God, who provides the transformational possibilities of wholeness and soundness wherever the community lives and works.
- *Shalom* brings a concern about the material and physical well-being of people. "Shalom" seekers are as concerned about the social and relational aspects of life as they are about reconciliation with God. They realize the two go hand in hand.
- *Shalom* nurtures trust, confidence, and mutual concern between neighbors. It is most evident when people live with a healthy

mutual concern for one another. The idea of "love your neighbor as you love yourself" is crucial to this aspect of shalom.
- *Shalom* takes place in the missional fields of the workplace and neighborhood. We are called to offer our work and our relationships to the glory of God.

We "shalom" our neighbors by taking them seriously and by participating with them. Choosing to be absent from these places allows everything but shalom to be present. If salt was used as a preservative for meat and the meat goes bad, you do not blame the meat, you blame the preservative. Our subtle lack of involvement with our neighbor and our insular subculture way of life in the church says, "We really don't care at all about the people or the society."

Bon Voyage!

The church offers a glimpse of God's upside-down kingdom, where the least shall be greatest, where the poor shall be rich, and where those without hope become those whose praises rise to heaven. Here the sinner finds not condemnation but forgiveness, and the outsider finds not a cold shoulder but a warm heart. Here, and here alone, those who in the eyes of the world are nothing find the light and affirmation of God shining upon them.

The greatest secret of the Christian faith is the community of faithfully gathered people we call the local church. At its best, when it lives with risky abandon in the borderlands, there is nothing like it on the face of the earth. This risky living moves the church from the margins back into the center of people's lives. An exciting movement is emerging as many churches around North America, facing the challenge of missional living, are moving out with incredible courage. Small or large, they are choosing to live differently, moving outside of the relative comforts of the walls of their churches into the wild and wonderful borderlands where faith is challenged and grown.

One of the important borderland events that our congregation has entered into is known as the "Party in the Park." It is an event that politicians and community organizers cannot afford to miss because it gathers people in ways that seldom occur at any other time in the year. Municipal, provincial, and national politicians all keep the date in their calendar. To miss it would be considered a great mistake because community members have come to expect their presence.

A young high school graduate and his family had their first encounter with our church at the "Party in the Park." Other events and encounters with people in our church took place along the way, but they all led to a point in which faith was accessed and nurtured. I cannot help watching him on Sunday mornings as he works a room of young people that look up to him, runs the projector for worship, and occasionally preaches with the hopeful words that only the young can utter with sincerity. His genuineness confirms that God blesses us when we choose to live in the borderlands. Life happens, and faithful living does breed new life and faith in others.

A REST STOP ALONG THE WAY

- What are ways for your congregation to begin the journey to the borderland?
- Many borderland churches begin the journey by introducing themselves to the community. Try asking some simple questions, such as: "Which places in our community or neighborhoods are we being called to engage? How will we introduce ourselves? What are the hindrances that block us from being able to engage?"

Appendix A

Song in the Borderland

A Seven-week Journey

Canadian Baptist Ministries, the organization I presently lead, has developed study materials to help congregations become both aware of their missional task and their neighborhood by using the borderland theme. Written by Brian Craig, a pastor in Canada and former colleague of mine, *The Song in the Borderland* is a learning resource designed to lead Christians to a deeper understanding of their role in reaching their community and world for Jesus Christ.

During a seven-week period, *The Song in the Borderland* explores creative new approaches to "singing the song" of God's love as well as introducing the powerful concept of "borderlands." Its purpose is to help congregations clarify the context for mission, both local and global. The material is biblically based and the approach is innovative, with an emphasis on interaction and hands-on experimentation.

The Song in the Borderland package includes:

- DVD with teaching segments
- Leader's Guide with sermon and worship resources
- Study Guides for small groups

Material can be ordered by phone or e-mail
Canadian Baptist Ministries: 905-821-3533
http://www.cbmin.org

Appendix B

Getting to Know Your Neighborhood

You may get to know your neighborhood in many ways, but the journey begins by defining the boundaries. Such boundaries represent the "bite-size chunk" that God is calling you to be responsible for. They enable you to find focus and clarity.

Once you have defined the boundaries, there are a number of ways to go about learning about the community. The least-effective method, but easiest to do, is a *basic demographic census.* Census and demographic studies are a regular occurrence undertaken by various business and social agencies and offer numbers and trends regarding age breakdown and other quantitative measurements of community. However, they don't give you faces and the subtleties that make neighborhoods unique.

The government also conducts demographic studies. This information gives an accessible analysis of communities. In many centers, especially in urban concentrations, it is possible to find departments within the municipality that contain neighborhood fact sheets, which break down the census characteristics. They may also be found online.

Another method of discovery is finding *key informants* who have lived in the area for a long time. They will know the local history. The limitations are obvious, but their narratives are often helpful.

Many churches have entered into *survey sampling.* Using questions either formulated by themselves or by a professional survey provider, church members go door to door along the streets, asking people a set of questions that the church members believe will help them understand the perceptions these people have of the church, faith, and religion in general. Unfortunately, these surveys have been misused and, while they can be helpful, they do not move the church members into any genuine relationship building or social interactions.

Nothing replaces *face-to-face interaction* and *social networking.* The most helpful information and understanding will always come from these encounters, especially if you enter into the process with adventure and hopefulness. Along with relationship building, a number of activities may facilitate observation and analysis. These activities are based on a key principle:

People themselves give the most helpful information, so why not engage them in good conversation?

Attend special community activities:

- Youth events, ball game, school drama, etc.
- Neighborhood celebrations, political events, garage sales, bazaars
- Community organization meetings for action

Establish the physical boundaries:

- The concept of the *church scattered* and the *church gathered* enables a congregation to focus and strategize on specific areas of relationships and natural networks.
- *Church gathered* is the neighborhood and context in which a particular church is situated. It is literally the place where God has placed your building and for which you have a responsibility. It is a unique placement.
- *Church scattered* is the neighborhoods and networks of relationship that take place when the congregation is spread out throughout the area. It includes workplaces, residential communities, social networks, and even global connections.

Investigate the common name of your neighborhood:

- What do people call this neighborhood? How did it come by this name and is it different than the official name given by the municipality? What does it tell you about this community?
- How do other people who live outside of the community perceive this neighborhood? Is that perception fair and accurate?

Walk it, drive it, and ride it:

- During three distinct periods of the day, travel the public transit system. Observe the various people groups you encounter. Who are they? Where are they going? Talk to them.
- Divide the day into these three sections and share the adventure amongst yourselves:
  ~ 8 a.m. to noon
  ~ 5 p.m. to 9 p.m.
  ~ 9 p.m. to midnight

Observe and record the following:

- What kind of churches, schools, and buildings do you see?
- What types of businesses do you see? Are there service shops, commercial areas? Are these stores recognizable name-brand

stores? Independent stores? Are new businesses moving into the neighborhood?

- What kind of industry is in the neighborhood? Do people who live in the neighborhood work in the neighborhood?
- If there are malls, how would you describe their condition? What types of commercial stores are represented here? Are stores closing down or do they appear to be stable? Have they changed in the last few years? What new ones have come into the community?
- What are the social gathering areas in the community (e.g., bars, sports clubs, parks)? If there are parks, in what condition are they? When are these social areas busiest?
- How would you describe the type of housing in your neighborhood? What kind of housing is it? (e.g., high-rise luxury condos, single family dwellings, walk-ups, rental apartments, etc.)
  - ~ What is the condition of the housing?
  - ~ What is the condition and presence of public facilities?
  - ~ What type of transportation do most people use?
  - ~ Is there a predominant ethnicity or socioeconomic class in the area? Is it changing or has it stayed stable in the last five years?
  - ~ How many social groups can you observe? Name them (e.g., elderly, young mothers, gangs, young families, age groupings, etc.)
- What are some the stated issues in this community? Resources?
- Who are the obvious leaders?
- What types of social service systems are present in the community? Name them. Introduce yourselves to them. Talk to them.
  - ~ Are there self-help groups that meet in the community? What are they? Where do they meet? Do people come from the community or from outside of the community?
  - ~ Is there any evidence of deterioration or regentrification in the community? What is new?

Walk the community and look into the faces:

- What do you see?
- What do you feel?
- Who do you see?

If you feel that a survey would be helpful, then put one together.

Surveys are simply lists of questions you would like to have answered. Avoid using "loaded" questions and using lengthy surveys. Answers to the questions should take no more than five minutes. Here are some cautions about surveys:

- Are the facts already available elsewhere?
- Is a survey likely to substitute for action?
- Do you have the resources to conduct a survey?
- Does the survey attempt to get at community issues and concerns or merely your own?

Here are some steps that can be taken when implementing a survey:

- Determine scope and size.
- Consider the fiscal and human costs.
- Organize a survey committee.
- Prepare survey forms.
- Prepare workers.
- Follow up on findings

APPENDIX C

Neighborhoods Are Different

Different neighborhoods require different strategies for engagement. See if you can identify the kind of neighborhood you are in from the list below and then reflect on how these characteristics impact strategy building for engagement. What will the challenges be? What are the natural places of engagement?

The connected community: In this community, individuals are in close contact and share many of the same concerns. They participate in shared activities within the larger community and have a sense of commonality.

The insular community: This neighborhood can be difficult to engage simply because it has a tight homogeneous character. It has a strong identity often based on ethnic frameworks and is self-contained, often functioning independent of the larger community. It has an amazing ability to screen out what does not conform to its ways.

The distributed community: This community also has a homogeneous character with many characteristics in common but it has very little active internal life. It is not tied to the larger community but neighbors do very little together in the way of activities. High-rise condominium dwellers are often a part of this type of community. These people made a particular decision to live a certain lifestyle of which one characteristic is anonymity.

The transitional community: These neighborhoods are involved in a game of "musical chairs." People enter these areas in a state of transition but are very active together until they move on. Often these communities have housing that allows for new immigrants or new homeowners, but their move into the neighborhood was never intended to be permanent. It was always perceived as a stepping stone. Communities such as this change in their makeup every four to five years.

The changeover community: These neighborhoods are in the middle of some kind of transformation. The changes may be in population or housing products. These communities are often fractured into clusters of people and interests with little, if any, commonality. Therefore, they lack cohesion. Often the old-timers, people who have been part of the neighborhood for a long time, perceive the newcomers as interlopers. The short-term future in this type of neighborhood will be fractured and tense, but, at some point, the transition will take place.

Appendix D

The Three "Ls" of Learning about Your Community

Look Back

- Study the general history of the community and the church. What are some of the interesting themes that give this community its character and ethos?
- Why was this community started? Are those needs still at work? Are there particular names associated with this history? Major turning points?
- What are some of the issues that arose in this community's history? How were they dealt with? Do some of these issues still appear to be at work?
- Are there people still residing in this community or neighborhood who were here at the beginning? Are any of them part of the church?

Look Around

- Study the statistical trends of the community. What types of people make up this community? Are there changes taking place that will make this community very different in the next five years? Are there distinct communities or sub-groups within the neighborhood?
- Which groups are most influential in this community? Are there particular individuals who have influence? Who are the political figures in this community?
- What are the new types of commercial properties in this neighborhood? Are there new businesses moving in? What are they? Where are the social service agencies situated?
- Are there churches that have particular influence in this community? Parachurch ministries? Nonprofit organizations?
- Go to a park and sit there for a few hours. What do you observe? Do the people in the park appear to know one another?
- Does your church look like the community? Why or why not?
- Do people in the church live in the neighborhood?

Look Ahead

- Explore all the possibilities of connecting with the community that emerge from the information you have gathered. Brainstorm possibilities that are framed in the following way: "If nothing prevented us from reaching out to engage this community, would we?
- Of all the suggestions, what would be the most natural and easiest one to do first? How can we make it happen?
- What activities would require more complex planning? Does the congregation have the resources to do them?
- What group in your community represents the make up of your congregation?

Appendix E

Questions to Be Asked in the Community in Which You Live and/or in Which Your Church Is Situated

1. What does this community feel like? *(Describe)*
2. What are the key issues in your community? Who can tell you about them?
3. Who are the people that make up this community? What are the socioeconomic characteristics? What size and kind of families live near the church?
4. How has it changed in the last ten years? Five years?
5. Does our church represent the demographic make up of our community? Why or why not? (Take out the hard numbers from a demographic study and compare them to your congregational profile.)
6. What are the rhythms of this community? When do people appear to be around? What are the times when people are most evident (actually visible outside of their residences)? How do they travel outside of their community? Where do their children go to school?
7. How do things get communicated in this community? When? Where?
8. What is the community's perception of our church? Of Christians, in general?
9. How can we create portals of engagement with the church?
10. What is the good news for people in this community?

Appendix F

Sampling of Helpful Web Sites for Your Borderland Discussions

www.thecolumbiapartnership.org

The Columbia Partnership is a community of Christian leaders seeking to transform the capacity of Christ-followers in churches, denominations, corporations, and schools to pursue and sustain vital Christ-centered ministry. They provide coaching, consulting, speaking, presenting of seminars/learning experiences, future planning, publications, networking, and brokering of knowledge and services. They seek to develop the capacities of leaders and organizations for learning, change, and transformation.

www.allelon.org/main.cfm

Allelon calls itself "A Movement of Missional Leaders," and its Web site provides helpful resources, conversations, and articles in a desire to stimulate missional church life.

Allelon says that its overarching mission is to educate and encourage the church to become a people among whom God can live, who will work as sign, symbol, and foretaste of his redeeming love and grace in their neighborhoods and the whole of society–ordinary women and men endeavoring to participate in God's mission to reclaim and restore the whole of creation and to bear witness to the world of a new way of being human.

http://emergentcanada.blogspot.com/2006/02/getting-to-know-us.html

Emergent Canada desires to facilitate inclusive conversations and partnerships among Canadians searching for authentic Christian faith through a missional life of love, justice, and beauty.

http://www.msainfo.org/

Mustard Seed Associates *(MSA)* provides resources and a network for other committed Christians to anticipate the future, decode the culture, convey the kingdom of God, and create new ways to be a difference and make a difference. They work to *inspire, connect, and create* in order to fulfill the mission. Believing God is changing the world through mustard seeds, MSA seeks to unleash the creative potential of ordinary people to make a difference in their *communities and in a world of urgent need.*

Appendix G

Further Reading Possibilities

On Being a People in Mission

Augsburger, David. *Dissident Discipleship: A Spirituality of Self-Surrender, Love of God and Love of Neighbor.* Grand Rapids: Brazos Press, 2006.

Bevans, Stephen. *Models of Contextual Theology: Faith and Cultures.* Maryknoll, N.Y.: Orbis Books, 1992.

Bibby, Reginald. *Unknown Gods: The Ongoing Story of Religion in Canada.* Toronto: Stoddart, 1993.

______. *There's Got to Be More! Connecting Churches & Canadians.* Winfield: Wood Lake Books, 1995.

______. *The Bibby Report: Social Trends Canadian Style.* Toronto: Stoddart, 1995.

Bosch, David J. *Transforming Mission: Paradigm Shifts in Theology of Mission.* Maryknoll, N.Y.: Orbis Books, 1991.

Brueggemann, Walter. *Cadences of Home: Preaching Among Exiles.* Louisville: Westminster John Knox Press, 1997.

Clemens, Semak. *Doing Local Theology.* Maryknoll, N.Y.: Orbis Books, 2002.

Fitch, David E. *The Great Giveaway: Reclaiming the Mission of the Church.* Grand Rapids: Baker Books, 2005.

Grenz, Stanley. *A Primer on Postmodernism.* Grand Rapids: Wm B. Eerdmans,, 1995.

Guder, Darrell, ed. *Missional Church: A Vision for the Sending of the Church in North America.* Grand Rapids: Wm. B. Eerdmans,, 1998.

Hunsberger, George. *Church Between Gospel and Culture: The Emerging Mission in North America.* Grand Rapids: Wm B. Eerdmans, 1996.

Long, Jimmy. *Emerging Hope: A Strategy for Reaching Postmodern Generations.* Downers Grove, Ill.: InterVarsity Press, 2004.

Minatrea, Milfred. *Shaped by God's Heart: The Passion and Practices of Missional Churches.* San Francisco: Jossey-Bass, 2004.

Newbigin, Lesslie. *Foolishness to the Greeks: The Gospel and Western Culture.* Grand Rapids: Wm B. Eerdmans, 1986.

______. *The Gospel in a Pluralist Society.* Grand Rapids: Wm. B. Eerdmans, 1989.

______. *Truth to Tell: The Gospel as Public Truth.* Grand Rapids: Wm B. Eerdmans, 1991.

______. *The Open Secret: An Introduction to the Theology of Mission.* Grand Rapids: Wm B. Eerdmans, 1995.

Posterski, Don. *True to You: Living Our Faith in Our Multi-Minded World.* Winfield: Woodlake Books, 1995.

Schrieter, Robert. *Constructing Local Theologies.* Maryknoll, N.Y.: Orbis Books, 1985.

Van Engen, Charles. *God's Missionary People: Rethinking the Purpose of the Local Church.* Grand Rapids: Baker Books, 1991.

Van Gelder, Craig. *Confident Witness–Changing World: Rediscovering the Gospel in North America.* Grand Rapids: Wm B. Eerdmans, 1999.

Wilson, Jonathan. *Living Faithfully in a Fragmented World.* Philadelphia: Trinity Press International, 1997.

On Being the Church

Clapp, Rodney. *A Peculiar People: The Church as Culture in a Post-Christian Society.* Downers Grove, Ill.: InterVarsity Press, 1996.

Dawn, Marva. *The Hilarity of Community: Romans 12 and How to Be the Church.* Grand Rapids: Wm B. Eerdmans, 1992.

Dulles, Avery. *Models of the Church.* Garden City, N.Y.: Doubleday and Co., Inc., 1974.

Frost, Michael. *The Shape of Things To Come: Innovation and Mission for the 21st Century Church.* Peabody, Mass.: Hendrickson, 2000.

Grenz, Stanley. *Created for Community.* Wheaton, Ill.: BridgePoint/Victor Books, 1996.

______. *Theology for the Community of Faith.* Nashville: Broadman & Holman, 1994.

Guder, Darrell. *Continuing Conversion of the Church.* Grand Rapids: Wm B. Eerdmans, 2002.

Hall, Douglas John. *The Future of the Church.* Toronto: UCPH, 1989.

Hauerwas, Stanley, and William Willimon. *Resident Aliens.* Nashville: Abingdon Press, 1989.

Leddy, Mary Jo. *Reweaving Religious Life.* Mystic, Conn.: Twenty-Third Publications, 1990.

Murray, Stuart. *Post-Christendom: Church and Mission in a Strange New World.* Carlisle, U.K.: Paternoster, 2004.

Posterski, Don, and Gary Nelson. *Future Faith Churches: Reconnecting with the Power of the Gospel for the 21st Century.* Winfield: Wood Lake Books, 1997.

Sweet, Leonard. *The Church in Emerging Culture: Five Perspectives.* Grand Rapids: Zondervan, 2003.

Van Gelder, Craig. *The Essence of the Church.* Grand Rapids: Baker, 2000.

Vanier, John. *Community & Growth.* New York: Paulist Press, 1979.

Watson, David. *I Believe in the Church.* London: Hodder and Stoughton, 1979.

Webber, Robert. *The Younger Evangelicals.* Grand Rapids: Baker Books, 2002.

Webster, Douglas. *Selling Jesus: What's Wrong with Marketing the Church.* Downers Grove, Ill.: InterVarsity Press, 1992.

Willimon, William. *The Intrusive Word: Preaching to the Unbaptized.* Grand Rapids: Wm B. Eerdmans, 1994.

Wright, N.T. *Bringing the Church to the World.* Minneapolis: Bethany House, 1992.

On Engaging through Word-Evangelism

Brueggemann, Walter. *Biblical Perspectives on Evangelism: Living in a Three-Storied Universe.* Nashville: Abingdon Press, 1993.

Gibbs, Eddie. *In Name Only: Tackling the Problem of Nominal Christianity.* Wheaton, Ill.: BridgePoint Book, 1994.

Green, Michael. *Evangelism Through the Local Church.* Nashville: Thomas Nelson, 1992.

Hunter, George. *How to Reach Secular People.* Nashville: Abingdon Press, 1992.

Pannell, William. *Evangelism from the Bottom Up.* Grand Rapids: Zondervan, 1992.

Posterski, Don. *Reinventing Evangelism: New Strategies for Tomorrow's Church.* Downers Grove, Ill.: InterVarsity Press, 1993.

Roxburgh, Alan. *Reaching a New Generation: Strategies for Tomorrow's Church.* Downers Grove, Ill.: InterVarsity Press, 1993.

Sider, Ronald J. *One-Sided Christianity: Uniting the Church to Heal a Lost and Broken World.* New York: HarperCollins, 1993.

Watson, David. *I Believe in Evangelism.* Grand Rapids: Wm B. Eerdmans, 1976.

On Engaging through Deed

Grigg, Viv. *Companion to the Poor.* Monrovia, Calif.: MARC, 1991.

______. *Cry of the Urban Poor.* Monrovia, Calif.: MARC, 1992.

Hauerwas, Stanley. *In Good Company: The Church as Polis.* Notre Dame: University of Notre Dame Press, 1995.

Linthicum, Robert. *City of God, City of Satan: A Biblical Theology of the Urban Church.* Grand Rapids: Zondervan, 1991.

______. *Empowering the Poor: Community Organizing Among the City's "Rag, Tag and Bobtail."* Monrovia, Calif.: MARC, 1991.

McKnight, John. *The Careless Society: Community and Its Counterfeits.* New York: Basic Books, 1995.

Sine, Tom. *The Mustard Seed Conspiracy.* Waco: Word Books, 1981.

Living Missionally

Dawn, Marva J. *Reaching Out without Dumbing Down: A Theology of Worship for the Turn of the Century.* Grand Rapids: Wm B. Eerdmans, 1995.

Frost, Michael, *Exiles: Living Missionally in a Post-Christian Culture.* Peabody, Mass.: Hendrickson, 2006.

Kidd, Sue Monk. *When the Heart Waits: Spiritual Direction for Life's Sacred Questions.* New York: HarperCollins, 1990.

Mulholland, M. R. *Invitation to a Journey: A Road Map for Spiritual Formation.* Downers Grove, Ill.: InterVarsity Press, 1993.

Peterson, Eugene. *The Contemplative Pastor: Returning to the Art of Spiritual Direction.* Grand Rapids: Wm B. Eerdmans, 1993 (reprint).

Willard, Dallas. *Renovation of the Heart: Putting on the Character of Christ.* Colorado Springs: NavPress, 2002.

Missioning Your Vocation

Banks, Robert. *Faith Goes to Work.* New York: The Alban Institute, 1993.
Diehl, William E. *The Monday Connection.* New York: HarperCollins, 1991.
Nouwen, Henri. *In the Name of Jesus.* New York: Crossroads, 1989.
Palmer, Parker. *The Active Life.* New York: HarperCollins, 1990.
Van Engen, Charles. *God So Loves the City: Seeking a Theology for Urban Mission.* Monrovia, Calif.: MARC, 1994.

On Leading

Armour, Michael. *Systems-Sensitive: Empowering Diversity Without Polarizing the Church.* Joplin, Mo.: College Press, 1995.
Bono, Edward. *Six Thinking Hats.* New York: Penguin Books, 1985.
Callahan, Kennon. *Effective Church Leadership.* New York: Harper & Row, 1990.
Clinton, Robert. *The Making of a Leader: Recognizing the Lessons and Stages of Leadership Development.* Colorado Springs: NavPress, 1988.
Collins, Jim. *Good to Great: Why Some Companies Make the Leap… and Others Don't.* New York: HarperCollins, 2001.
Cosgrove, Charles. *Church Conflict: The Hidden Systems Behind the Fights.* Nashville: Abingdon Press, 1994.
De Pree, Max. *Leadership Is an Art.* Garden City, N.Y.: Doubleday and Co. Inc., 1989.
Friedman, Edwin. *Generation to Generation: Family Process in Church and Synagogue.* New York: Guildford, 1985.
______.*A Failure of Nerve: Leadership in the Age of the Quick Fix.* The Edwin Friedman Estate/Trust, 1999.
Gibb, Eddie. *Leadership Next.* Downers Grove, Ill.: InterVarsity Press, 2005.
Kotter, John. *Leading Change.* Boston: Harvard Business School Press, 1996.
Neuhaus, R. J. *Freedom for Ministry.* Grand Rapids: Wm. B. Eerdmans, 1992 (reprint).
Peterson, Eugene. *Working the Angles: The Shape of Pastoral Integrity.* Grand Rapids: Wm B. Eerdmans, 1987.
Roxburgh, Alan, and Fred Romanuk. *The Missional Leader: Equipping Your Church to Reach a Changing World.* San Francisco: Jossey Bass, 2006.
Schaef, Ann W. *The Addictive Organization.* New York: Harper and Row, 1988.
Van Oech, Roger. *A Kick in the Seat of the Pants.* New York: Harper & Row, 1986.

Notes

Introduction

[1]David E. Fitch, *The Great Giveaway: Reclaiming the Mission of the Church* (Grand Rapids: Baker Books, 2005).

[2]Mark Buchanan, *Your God Is Too Safe* (Sisters, Oreg.: Multnomah, 2001).

[3]Gloria Anzaldúa, *Borderlands/La Frontera: The New Mestiza* (San Francisco: Anne Lute Books, 1987; 2d ed., 1999).

[4]Henry Giroux, *Border Crossings: Cultural Workers and the Politics of Education* (New York: Routledge, 1992).

[5]Charles Van Engen, *God's Missionary People: Rethinking the Purpose of the Local Church* (Grand Rapids: Baker Books, 1991), 165.

Chapter 1: Learning to Sing the Song

[1]John Kotter, *Leading Change* (Boston: Harvard Business School Press, 1996).

[2]G. K. Chesterton, *The Everlasting Man* (New York: Dodd, Mead, 1925), from the chapter, "The Man in the Cave," available online at http://www.mrrena.com/misc/em.shtml.

[3]See Stephen Covey, *First Things First* (New York: Simon & Schuster, 1994).

[4]Rick Warren, *The Purpose Driven Life: What Am I Here For?* (Grand Rapids: Zondervan, 2003), 17.

[5]Eddie Gibbs, *Leadership Next* (Downers Grove, Ill.: InterVarsity Press, 2005), 12.

Chapter 2: Crossing Over

[1]See John Hamlin, *Inheriting the Land* (Grand Rapids: Wm B. Eerdmans,, 1983).

[2]Roger Van Oech, *Whack on the Side of the Head* (New York: Harper and Row, 1986), writing about creativity.

[3]Mike Regele, *The Death of the Church* (Zondervan: Grand Rapids, 1995,) 23–24.

[4]Jonathan Wilson, *Why Church Matters: Worship, Ministry and Mission in Practice* (Grand Rapids: Brazos Press, 2006), 21.

[5]Darrell Guder, *Missional Church: A Vision for the Sending of the Church in North America* (Grand Rapids: Wm B. Eerdmans, 1998), 1–3.

[6]Ibid., 4.

[7]See the writings of people such as Leonard Sweet, Al Roxburgh, Michael Frost, Brian McLaren, and many others.

[8]Eddie Gibbs and Ryan Bolger, *Emerging Churches: Creating Christian Community in Postmodern Cultures* (Grand Rapids: Baker Books, 2006).

[9]Steve Collins, as quoted in ibid.

[10]Leonard Sweet, as quoted in an Associated Baptist Press news release, February 6, 2007.

[11]Ibid.

[12]Lesslie Newbigin, *Gospel for a Pluralist Society* (Grand Rapids: Wm B. Eerdmans, 1990) and *Foolishness to the Greeks* (Grand Rapids: Wm B. Eerdmans, 1986).

[13]David Bosch, *Transforming Mission: Paradigm Shifts in Theology of Mission* (Maryknoll, N.Y.: Orbis Books, 1991.)

[14]Gibbs and Bolger, *Emerging Churches,* 52.

[15]Samuel Escobar, *The New Global Mission: The Gospel from Everywhere to Everyone* (Downers Grove, Ill., InterVarsity Press: 2003), 88.

Chapter 3: Recovering Our Roots

[1]Jimmy Long, *Emerging Hope: A Strategy for Reaching Postmodern Generations* (Downers Grove, Ill.: InterVarsity Press, 2004), 99.

[2]David Augsburger, *Dissident Discipleship: A Spirituality of Self-Surrender, Love of God and Love of Neighbor* (Grand Rapids: Brazos Press, 2006), 75.

[3]David Fitch, *The Great Giveaway: Reclaiming the Mission of the Church* (Grand Rapids: Baker Books, 2005), 56.

[4]Philip D. Kenneson and James L. Street, *Selling Out the Church* (Eugene, Oreg.: Cascade Books, 1997), 156–57.

[5]Stanley Hauerwas and William Willimon, *Resident Aliens* (Nashville: Abingdon Press, 1989), 46–47.

[6]Avery Dulles, *Models of the Church* (Garden City, N.Y.: Doubleday and Co., 1974).

[7]Stanley J. Grenz, *Created for Community* (Wheaton, Ill.: BridgePoint/Victor Books, 1996), 209.

[8]Walter Brueggemann, *Cadences of Home: Preaching Among Exiles* (Louisville: Westminster John Knox Press, 1997), 209.

[9]Darrell Guder, *Missional Church: A Vision for the Sending of the Church in North America* (Grand Rapids: Wm. B. Eerdmans, 1998).

[10]Ibid., 11.

[11]Ibid., 6.

[12]Robert Webber, *The Younger Evangelicals: Facing the Challenges of the New World* (Grand Rapids: Baker Books, 2002), 133.

[13]Lesslie Newbigin, *One Body, One Gospel, One World: The Christian Mission Today* (London: Paternoster, 1958), 21, 43.

[14]These two marvelous theologians gave me these words in their addresses, which I was privileged to hear: Marva at the IVCF Canada National Staff Conference, 2001, and Mary Jo four months after September 11 at the National Staff Conference of the Canadian Salvation Army, 2002.

Chapter 4: Landscapes and Tool Kits

[1]Eugene Peterson, *Under the Unpredictable Plant: An Exploration in Vocational Holiness* (Grand Rapids: Wm. B. Eerdmans, 1992), 14.

[2]Jeff Woods, *Congregational Megatrends* (New York: The Alban Institute, 1996), 103.

[3]Irwin Barker and Don Posterski, *Where's a Good Church?* (Winfield, B.C.: Woodlake Books, 1995).

[4]Loren Mead, *The Once and Future Church* (New York: The Alban Institute, 1991), 53.

[5]Edwin H. Friedman, *A Failure of Nerve: Leadership in the Age of the Quick Fix* (The Edwin Friedman Estate/Trust, 1999.)

[6]Mike Regele, *The Death of the Church* (Grand Rapids: Zondervan, 1995), 206.

[7]Leonard Hjalmarson, quoted from a *Christianity Today* Web article entitled "Kingdom Leadership in the Postmodern Era," www.christianity.ca/church/leadership/2005/05.000.html

[8]Clay Shirsky, quoted in ibid.

[9]For an analysis on Christendom and its decline, refer to the books on missional church life in the bibliography.

[10]James Engel and William Dryness, *Changing the Mind of Missions: Where Have We Gone Wrong?* (Downers Grove, Ill.: InterVarsity Press, 2000).

[11]Friedman, *A Failure of Nerve.*

[12]Ibid., 13.

[13]Ibid.

[14]Gordon Macdonald, *The Life God Blesses: Weathering the Storms of Life that Threaten the Soul* (Nashville: Thomas Nelson, 1994).

[15]Marva J. Dawn and Eugene Peterson, *The Unnecessary Pastor: Rediscovering the Call* (Grand Rapids: Wm. B. Eerdmans, 1998), 15.

[16]Don Posterski and Gary Nelson, *Future Faith Churches: Reconnecting with the Power of the Gospel for the 21st Century* (Winfield, B.C.: Wood Lake Books, 1997).

[17]Macdonald, *The Life God Blesses,* xii.

[18]Lee Bolman and Terence Deal, *Leading with Soul: An Uncommon Journey of the Spirit* (San Francisco, Jossey Bass: 1995), 39.

[19]Jimmy Long, *Emerging Hope: A Strategy for Reaching Postmodern Generations* (Downers Grove, Ill.: InterVarsity Press, 2004), 134.

[20]Jim Collins, *Good to Great: Why Some Companies Make the Leap and Others Don't* (New York: HarperCollins, 2001).

[21]James M. Burns, *Leadership* (New York, Harper and Row, 1978).

[22]Charles Van Engen, *God's Missionary People: Rethinking the Purpose of the Local Church* (Grand Rapids: Baker Books, 1991), 165.

[23]Alan Roxburgh and Fred Romanuk, *The Missional Leader: Equipping Your Church to Reach a Changing World* (San Francisco: Jossey Bass, 2006.)

[24]Dallas Willard, "How Does the Disciple Live?" previously unpublished article available online at http://www.dwillard.org/articles/artview.asp?artID=103.

[25]Ibid.

[26]Leonard Hjalmarson, quoted from a *Christianity Today* Web article entitled "Kingdom Leadership in the Postmodern Era," www.christianity.ca/church/leadership/2005/05.000.html

[27]Peter Senge, "Communities of Leaders and Learners," *Harvard Business Review* (September-October, 1997; 75th anniversary issue).

Chapter 5: Herding Cats

[1]Alan Roxburgh and Fred Romanuk, *The Missional Leader: Equipping Your Church to Reach a Changing World* (San Francisco: Jossey Bass, 2006), 145.

[2]For a helpful resource on leadership see Max DePree, *Leadership Is an Art* (Garden City, N.Y.: Doubleday and Co., 1989).

[3]Martin Luther King Jr. as quoted in Richard J. Neuhaus, *Freedom for Ministry* (New York: Harper and Row, 1992) 13.

[4]Jimmy Long, *Emerging Hope: A Strategy for Reaching Postmodern Generations,* (Downers Grove, Ill.: InterVarsity Press, 2004), 99.

[5]Edgar Schein, *Organizational Culture and Leadership: A Dynamic View* (San Francisco: Jossey-Bass, 1992).

[6]David Bosch, *Transforming Mission: Paradigm Shifts in Theology of Mission* (Maryknoll, N.Y.: Orbis Books, 1991), 349.

[7]Roxburgh and Romanuk, *The Missional Leader.*

[8]From a blog article by Alan Roxburgh, Spring 2005, www.allenon.org

[9]Ibid.

[10]William Easum, *Sacred Cows Make Gourmet Burgers* (Nashville: Abingdon Press, 1995), 99.

[11]Jonathan Wilson, *Why Church Matters: Worship, Ministry and Mission in Practice* (Grand Rapids: Brazos Press, 2006), 153.

[12]See books such as George Bullard's *Pursuing the Full Kingdom Potential of Your Congregation* (St. Louis: Lake Hickory Resources, 2005) and other books that are part of the TCP Leadership Series through Chalice Press.

[13]Anne Lamott, *Traveling Mercies* (Garden City, N.Y.: Doubleday and Co., 2000.)

Chapter 6: Missioning the Church

[1]William Diehl, *The Monday Connection* (New York: HarperCollins, 1991).

[2]Robert Webber, *The Younger Evangelicals: Facing the Challenges of the New World* (Grand Rapids: Baker Books, 2002), 240–41.

[3]Lesslie Newbigin, quoted in ibid., 103.

[4]William Willimon, *The Intrusive Word: Preaching to the Unbaptized* (Grand Rapids: Wm. B. Eerdmans,, 1994), 2.

[5]George Hunsberger in *Missional Church: A Vision for the Sending of the Church in North America,* ed. D. Gruder (Grand Rapids: Wm. B. Eerdmans, 1998), 97, 106.

[6]David Augsburger, *Dissident Discipleship: A Spirituality of Self-Surrender, Love of God and Love of Neighbor* (Grand Rapids: Brazos Press, 2006), 9.

[7]Ronald Rolheiser, *A Holy Longing: The Search for a Christian Spirituality* (Garden City, N.Y.: Doubleday and Co., 1999.)

[8]Ibid., 173

[9]See Augsburger, *Dissident Discipleship.*

[10]Quoted from the *Letter to Diognetus.* A Christian named Quadratus wrote this document to Hadrian, the Emperor of Rome. It served as an "apologia" for Christians at that time.

[11]Robert Wuthnow, *Christianity in the 21st Century* (New York: Oxford Press, 1993).

[12]David Bosch, *Transforming Mission: Paradigm Shifts in Theology of Mission* (Maryknoll, N.Y.: Orbis Books, 1991), 367.

[13]Ibid., 356.

[14]Annie Dillard, *Teaching a Stone to Talk* (New York: HarperCollins, 1988), 60.

Chapter 7: Mapping the Journey

[1]Rodney Clapp, *A Peculiar People: The Church as a Culture in a Post-Christian Society* (Downers Grove, Ill., InterVarsity Press, 1996), 116.

[2]Randy Frazee, *The Connecting Church: Beyond Small Groups to Authentic Community* (Grand Rapids: Zondervan: 2001), 67.